'Christine Nixon and Amanda Sinclair have written a terrific book which contains great advice for women to own and manage our lives and careers. It should be compulsory reading for girls (and boys!) and for people of all ages. It doesn't aim to find one theory or "smart phrase" about women's lives, but, using humour and practical ideas, gives all of us insights into the issues women face as we navigate our way through life.'

Elizabeth Proust AO,
Chair of the Australian Institute of Company Directors

WOMEN LEADING

WOMEN LEADING

CHRISTINE NIXON
AND AMANDA SINCLAIR

MELBOURNE UNIVERSITY PRESS

MELBOURNE UNIVERSITY PRESS
An imprint of Melbourne University Publishing Limited
Level 1, 715 Swanston Street, Carlton, Victoria 3053, Australia
mup-info@unimelb.edu.au
www.mup.com.au

First published 2017
Text © Christine Nixon and Amanda Sinclair, 2017
Design and typography © Melbourne University Publishing Limited, 2017

This book is copyright. Apart from any use permitted under the *Copyright Act 1968* and subsequent amendments, no part may be reproduced, stored in a retrieval system or transmitted by any means or process whatsoever without the prior written permission of the publishers.

Every attempt has been made to locate the copyright holders for material quoted in this book. Any person or organisation that may have been overlooked or misattributed may contact the publisher.

Text design and typesetting by Megan Ellis
Cover design by Design by Committee
Printed in Australia by McPherson's Printing Group

National Library of Australia Cataloguing-in-Publication entry

Nixon, Christine, 1953– author.
Women leading/Christine Nixon, Amanda Sinclair.

Leadership in women.
Women executives.
Women—Social conditions.
Other Creators/Contributors: Sinclair, Amanda, 1953– author.

9780522871623 (paperback)
9780522871630 (ebook)

Includes index.

Contents

Introduction	vii
Part 1: Learning from women's leadership	**1**
1 Beginnings and collaborations	3
2 Lessons from the past	21
3 Where women are now	35
Part 2: Achieving	**49**
4 Twelve lessons in leading change	51
5 Leadership in difficult times	67
6 Influencing and enabling	86
7 Valuing conversations	99
8 'Hot coals' management	110
Part 3: Flourishing	**119**
9 Power: How to find it, use it and own it	121
10 Physicality: How women are seen as leaders and how they can respond	138
11 Understanding identities, stages and transitions	154
12 Managing and reducing risks	169
13 Resilience and renewal	183
14 Wise words from women	197
Looking forward and sustaining	211
Acknowledgements	215
Notes	217
Bibliography	227
Index	237

Introduction

If leadership is about initiating and mobilising change, we have much to learn from women. Throughout history and across societies and cultures, women have developed ways of challenging the status quo, of voicing their interests, and of influencing families, workplaces, communities and nations to become more humane, equitable and inclusive. Because of the intractability of obstacles, women have had to find ingenious pathways to influence and reliable means to sustain themselves and others when encountering setbacks. Women have had to maintain energy and spirit not just over lifetimes but also across generations.

We believe leadership by women has not been adequately recognised, and this book sets out to learn how, and to what ends, women lead. Both of us, Amanda and Christine, have grown frustrated at the narrow approaches that miss the rich diversity of women's leadership. Some research on business leadership paints women as 'not quite up to it'. The implication is that they require more experience as chief executive officers (CEOs) or in general management, need to 'lean in'[1] more, be more ambitious or claim credit for achievements. Based on our experience and research, we believe the opposite to be true. Women's skills, capacities, merit and leadership qualities exist but have not been acknowledged by mainstream writers as leaders to learn from. We want to change that: to throw the spotlight on how women have been and are leading, innovatively and sustainably, across a diverse range of contexts. Especially as agents of disruption and doing leadership differently, there is plenty to learn from women.

Women dominate the workforce in healthcare and hospitals, but there has been little research on the qualities of female leaders in this field, about their skills and strategies in leading massive, complex institutions. Women also have long track records of leading human services organisations and schools.[2] More recently, women have become prominent as local government mayors and chief executives, overseeing vast and complex operations delivering key community services.[3] Many women have provided outstanding political leadership during very troubled times—think of presidents Mary Robinson and Mary McAleese in Ireland, and Germany's Chancellor Angela Merkel. Julia Gillard, Australia's Prime Minister from 2010 to 2013, was on most counts an exceptional leader, with a track record of introducing significant reforms in education, disability and health policy and services, negotiating their successful passage despite leading a minority government.

Over the history of leadership studies, most research and writing has been undertaken by men. Writers about leadership derived lessons about how to lead initially from the military, then from bureaucracies that were designed, led and largely 'manned' by men, and more recently from corporations set up and dominated by men. What this has meant is that often those of us interested in learning about leadership simply miss seeing the leadership of women or are confronted by narrow views of leaders being either born for such roles, or of over-lionised male leaders saving the country, community or organisation.

INTRODUCTION

In writing this book we focus on, learn from, celebrate and support the leadership of women. It feels timely. During 2016, while we were working on this subject, a crop of new women political leaders emerged internationally. Rome elected its first woman mayor, Virginia Raggi, in its history. British conservatives elected a woman prime minister, Theresa May, only the second in their history. With the appointment of the first woman police commissioner of London's Metropolitan Police Service, women hold three of five top posts in the English criminal justice system. In Australia, the 2016 elections saw record numbers of women standing for and being elected to federal parliament, especially in the Australian Labor Party (ALP), which had committed to quotas of women being pre-selected. The ALP is ahead of its targets.[4] In other areas of public life there has also been recognition of women's leadership. In sports, for example, at both an elite level and a community one, women are lobbying successfully for more resources for women.[5] In other areas of activism, such as human rights, and in entrepreneurialism, women are driving change.

Yet there remain substantial obstacles to qualified women seeking leadership roles. In November 2016, despite the predictions of polls and winning a greater number of votes, Hillary Clinton was unsuccessful in her bid to become the first woman president of the United States.[6] Although her gender was arguably only one factor in the campaigns mounted against her by the successful candidate, Donald Trump, and other opponents, Clinton encountered a heightened level of gendered vilification and hatred. Observing that campaign is a sobering reminder of the deep discomfort many in society feel about having a woman in a position of power. Clinton, we believe, showed strong and convincing leadership but was 'Trumped' by a man far less qualified, a continuing and common phenomenon across many sectors and societies.

The insights and ideas we offer here have come from our observations about and our learning from women leaders, as well as our own experiences. The chapters cover issues, concepts, stories and research that, in our experience, people have found useful. Though largely about women, we believe men will also find these interesting.

It's just that we have set out to redress the imbalance in leadership books and focus our work on women, their experiences and what we can learn from them. We pay particular attention to dealing with aspects of leadership where many women have faced obstacles, not due to their qualities but to the cultures, structures and systems in which they are often working. These include issues such as scrutiny about how women look, behave and speak, and advice that they need to dress conservatively or deepen their voices to conform to masculine norms. Because of these obstacles, women's leadership has often had to be more disruptive and courageous, innovative and sustaining—vital ingredients for future leaders of both genders.

In *Women Leading*, we hope to challenge you to consider your own experiences and stories, the narratives you've been given and those you've taken on, and how and why you behave the way you do in leadership. We hope you'll reflect and add new self-insights and understandings from others to enhance your leadership and enjoy it more.

Part 1

LEARNING FROM WOMEN'S LEADERSHIP

1
Beginnings and collaborations

Women leaders are often forced by circumstance—by an unusual level of visibility and scrutiny, for example—to bring heightened levels of reflection and innovation to how they do their jobs.

Amanda Sinclair, 2007

The collaboration that underpins our work began in 2001. A mutual friend—a woman leading a large institution through difficult transitions—said to Amanda, 'You're interested in leadership and change management, you should talk to my friend Christine Nixon.' Christine was then working as Regional Police Commander for a large area of southern New South Wales. When she was successful in applying for and took up the job of Victoria's Police Commissioner in 2001, Amanda wrote to her, talked about the research she had done, and asked if they might meet. Keen to observe the way Christine was leading cultural and organisational reform within Victoria Police, Amanda knew well the scale of the challenge from conducting earlier work with Victoria Police under previous commissioners.

Amanda is an academic leader with a reputation as a pioneer in areas of leadership, change, gender, diversity and sexuality.

Her academic articles and books include *Doing Leadership Differently* (1998), *Leadership for the Disillusioned* (2007), which offers the argument that leadership should be aimed at freeing people, and *Leading Mindfully* (2016). Targeting her writing to practising leaders as well as researchers, Amanda has wanted to help people find innovative, enjoyable and sustainable ways to lead. As part of their work together, Amanda spent several weeks 'shadowing' Christine as she went about the daily business of leading Victoria Police. As their relationship developed, Christine asked for feedback on meetings and interactions, getting Amanda's sense of how her leadership was 'landing' in different circumstances.

Christine found this independent feedback useful: it helped her adapt behaviours and improve the effectiveness of particular interactions. The experience also ensured Christine became an advocate for having a colleague or friend observe and give feedback at work. From Amanda's perspective, it was remarkable to research a leader who was so open to learning and change. While senior police were initially taken aback to find themselves in high-level meetings with a researcher at the table, it soon became accepted as just part of the opening-up of the police and signalled that, right from the top, the culture was to be one of working with a wide range of community and stakeholders, including researchers, as partners in improving policing.

Christine first developed some of the material in this book, especially in Part 2, for a workshop for the Australia and New Zealand School of Government (ANZSOG). Some draws from *Fair Cop*, a book Christine wrote with Jo Chandler in 2011, and Christine's knowledge about women in leadership through her studies and years of experience. Both of us have worked with ANZSOG and together we further develop and teach the program that explores challenges facing women in leadership in the public sector. Our Women in Leadership program has been designed to allow women to share and validate their style of leadership—to be themselves. The workshop was piloted in 2011 and has been offered by ANZSOG ever since. Over 1500 women from Australia, New Zealand, Indonesia and Pacific nations have also undertaken it in shorter variations of the course.

As a 'women only' workshop, the program was initially controversial. A criticism was that women-only programs put the focus on women to 'fix' their own absence, to train them up to perform better in what are, in many cases, flawed leadership cultures, rather than to challenge and change those cultures. However, an all-women group enables a deeper exploration of the issues faced by women in leadership than a mixed-gender group typically allows—and we have both had much experience working on gender issues in mixed-gender groups. Further the women-only environment provides an opportunity to appreciate and celebrate the diversity of women, their experiences and their beliefs—participants often really hear the different experiences in a way that is powerful and becomes a particular feature of the learning environment.

Over the past decade there has been an explosion of academic and popular interest in women's leadership in Australia and globally. Yet we think there is a gap that we are seeking to fill. Our thinking offers a unique blend of leadership experience with academic research. In our separate roles—Christine leading police and the Bushfire Reconstruction and Recovery Authority, as a Director, Chair and Deputy University Chancellor, and as a sought-after speaker and advocate; Amanda as a professor, teacher and consultant—as well as in our work together, we have shared our ideas and practices with diverse groups of women. As you read you will hear our two distinctive voices and experience—Christine with her extensive leadership experience and practical, down-to-earth approach; Amanda with her understanding of research, and her work coaching and teaching in management education and helping leaders become more reflective and mindful. There are many areas where we agree but some others where we have different perspectives. Our intent here has been to let the experience and wisdom of women speak, as well as offer our own contributions and perspectives.

Getting to know you

Our work together continues to evolve, as we add new thinking and material in response to our own learning and listening to participants. What we do challenges people on several levels. It has a flow that has taken many participants by surprise. We have seen the workshop challenge the very core of some women's beliefs about leadership and themselves. It also strengthens and models the value of working in partnership—something we believe is vital for success in leadership. Women's experiences are diverse. There is no one way to be effective and flourish in leadership, but we are confident people learn, and can learn, much from each other. To that end, we wish to share our own histories and experiences because we believe it is pivotal for leaders to be prepared to do so.

Christine

In my memoir, *Fair Cop*, I describe my childhood as a rare time. The 1950s saw post-war parents trying to establish families, struggling to create stable and comfortable homes, and our family was no different. My dad Ross worked long hours and was away a great deal. I have an older brother, Len, and a younger one, Mark, born eleven years after me. My mother Betty worked when I was young and this was unusual. It made Len and me self-reliant and caused us both to grow up quickly and take on responsibilities. I was also part of a new community. The neighbours became family and still are. My father Ross is ninety and, after an amazing life, still lives in the same street where I grew up—sadly without Betty.

At age eighteen in 1971, I applied to join the NSW Police and joined the Police Academy as PW Probationary Constable No. 173 in October 1972. There were 130 women and 8000 men in the NSW Police. I rose through the ranks by both seniority and through positional promotion. As a deal with my father—he didn't want me to follow in his footsteps and join the force—I also commenced study, first at TAFE and then part-time at university. In 1984, and at the relatively low level of Senior Constable, I was awarded a Harkness Fellowship from the Commonwealth Fund of New York and went to Harvard University's Kennedy School of Government in the United

States and attained a Master of Public Administration. I then stayed on as a Research Fellow for a further year and travelled to thirty American states as part of the scholarship. I returned to the NSW Police in 1986 to continue my career and become, in 1994, the first woman Assistant Commissioner in New South Wales, and the second in Australia.

In 2001, with some encouragement from my father and my husband, John Becquet, I applied for the Chief Commissioner role in Victoria. Much to my surprise I was appointed to the position in April of that year and would retire in 2009. I was then invited to become Chair of the Victorian Bushfire Reconstruction and Recovery Authority after the devastating Victorian bushfires. In 2010, I completed that role and started a new phase of my career, including becoming a member of Monash University Council and then Deputy Chancellor, Chair of Monash College, a subsidiary of the university, and of Good Shepherd Microfinance. I am also an independent member of the Board of the Royal Australian College of General Practitioners, the Castlemaine State Festival and an adviser, mentor and speaker on leadership.

My long commitment to improving life for women and girls started back in the late 1960s. I found myself surrounded by many smart and talented women, whether in the Coles variety store where I worked part-time or at our church or in the community, none of whom were appointed to management roles when they were easily the best person for the job. It seemed like the women were the helpers—except they actually did the work! I was surrounded at the time by the rise of the feminist movement and read *The Female Eunuch* by Germaine Greer, realising along the way that the world was against women. Thus began my fight for equality that lasted through my thirty-seven years with the police, whether it was about expanding responsibilities, or arguing for maternity leave and part-time work, or for advancement and equality in promotions,

I had a drive to change the position for women. The work I began in the 1970s to improve police and community responses to family violence, child abuse and sexual assault continues and is just as needed today.

After my full-time role leading the Bushfire Reconstruction and Recovery Authority concluded I wondered what I might do next. It seemed I knew a lot about the position of women in society, about how to be successful as a woman and how to survive. And so, what began next was the phase of my life that led to me working with thousands of women who believe they can be leaders, who want to achieve and flourish.

Amanda

I share a birthday with Christine. Yes, we were born on the same day, same year—amazingly, the mutual friend who introduced us was also born on this day! My early childhood was during that period when the ideal was for women to devote themselves to motherhood and suburban 'domestic bliss'. I was the third born, after two brothers, both of whom took up a lot of my parents' time for different reasons. In response, I learned to be quiet, good and smart. School reports described me as 'conscientious', a word I came to intensely dislike because of the way it was used to downplay my, and other girls', intelligence as just the result of hard work and dutifulness.

Things changed dramatically when my father died. I was fifteen. My mum, who had gone back to university when her children were little—much to the disapproval of many neighbours and friends—started work as a teacher. Even though we struggled, we would have been very poor if Mum hadn't had that job. It was the dawning of second-wave feminism and our family was confronted with the reality that women needed to be financially independent. My consciousness about gender and the issues women faced at work and in leadership began to develop through my experiences after I graduated, working as a social planner, then a consultant, in male-dominated organisations, often the only woman apart from support staff. Later, as I was completing my PhD, I heard and saw firsthand the misogyny faced by women elected to local government.

I became an academic at the same time as I was caring for small children, trying to combine teaching and researching in the competitive and masculine environment of a business school.[1] The kinds of experiences I had would be familiar to many women readers who have worked with largely male groups of colleagues and students, many of whom believed that as a woman I had nothing of value to teach. I was kindly advised by one senior male that it was career suicide to specialise in gender research. Another suggested I must be 'imagining things' when I started to draw attention to the sexism that other women and I routinely faced in professional careers.

What saved me through this difficult period was the support and writing of women who validated my experiences, and helped me see that what I was encountering was not about me but about the structural circumstances of power. The reactions I was running up against were the inevitable ways that those with power hang on to it and attribute issues or reactions as a problem to the newcomer who looks different, rather than to recognise they may reveal bias or problems with the status quo.

For all these personal and professional reasons, I am committed to supporting women to pursue leadership in ways that work for them, not to feel they need to camouflage themselves or turn themselves into someone else to succeed. I also believe that ensuring women hear each other's stories is deeply and powerfully useful. It reminds us we are not alone. It helps us recognise and take advantage of support. It frees us up to see new paths and energises and inspires. While it gives me great satisfaction to encourage and advocate for all leaders wanting to have positive impacts, women, I believe, especially need recognition.

We will talk more about us, our successes and failures, our doubts and hopes, in the chapters that follow, as who you are is important. Just because you take up a formal leadership position, or seek to influence others through leading, you can't simply adopt a persona that has nothing to do with who you are underneath. Despite the pressures on leaders, and especially women leaders, to conform to heroic templates of leadership or to hide themselves behind professional masks, it is almost never the right path—for the individual or the quality and impact of their leadership.[2]

We begin our workshops by asking participants to introduce themselves—not with their job or organisation but by commenting on what their family or colleagues might say about them, what they might want the group to know about them, and to share any other information that would be useful while they are participating in the program. This process takes time but is also used to model a way of leading that requires the group and the leader to share information about themselves. Many of the participants are nervous at the beginning of the program, but they come to understand that they are not all that different from others in the group, including the leaders. The process also goes towards creating a trusting environment in which people can feel comfortable in sharing their experiences, their knowledge and perhaps their doubts and fears.

Taking the time to introduce yourself as a leader lets people know where you come from and what's important to you. Christine attended a conference recently where a group of high-level executive women were asked to share lessons from their past to assist those in the audience. One woman spoke of a major operation she had been involved in and shared her experience about managing a complex group. Another spoke of her history growing up poor with an abusive and alcoholic father and the risks and problems she faced and how she overcame them—that story was very moving and inspiring. On the other hand, another speaker just volunteered some technical challenges she was facing in her role. Offered the opportunity to share insights and then avoiding the challenge says a great deal about a person: a lack of openness, and perhaps even a lack of care in helping others rise to the top.

When Christine joined Victoria Police she took the opportunity at her swearing-in to give a speech to let the community know who she was and what was important to her.[3] It was later published and partly televised. The speech invited the broader community to understand something about her history, values and priorities. Christine said she had various roles that were important to who she was and, 'I won't be abandoning or compromising them'. She also stated:

> First, I am woman. Much has been and will continue to be made of the fact that I am the first woman Chief Commissioner ... The female gender has brought its fair share of brains and imagination to policing, and femininity has, I hope, helped to nourish the caring and compassionate values and ideals that have always been embedded in the core of good policing.
>
> Don't get me wrong. Don't misconstrue caring for others, wanting to help the disadvantaged, the needy, the distressed, the victim, as being soft or weak on any account ... Don't think that the feminine virtues mean being indifferent to those who cheat, steal from and commit violence on others. That kind of softness has never been associated with femininity—ask any mother!
>
> My motivation to become a police officer stemmed from my deep conviction for the need for a tough and uncompromising response to those whose behaviour threatens our wellbeing, our freedom, our peace of mind, and our property.[4]

Christine went on to describe her roles as citizen, spouse and police officer. They are the roles that 'make me the person I am', she said. Instilled in her by her parents, these roles were developed through the support of others and, she asserted, would deeply inform her leadership approach. After her speech, Christine reflected:

> I have come to the position along a path that many said was impossible. I want to tell you that more things are possible than you might think. What is required are faith and optimism in people. If you act on that, and don't settle for anything less, you won't end up compromising that greatness that could have been.[5]

Shaping the norms

In our workshops and teaching, we create opportunities to discuss the way in which the group might operate by asking questions. What kinds of principles and values underpin and guide the conduct of the group? How will individuals treat each other? While there is sometimes a sense of impatience, even cynicism, about the process, we have found it is invariably valuable on both a symbolic and practical level. This exercise sets the ground rules for the session and models a practice we think could be adopted in many workplaces. Explicitly stating how a meeting will be conducted, or inviting discussion from the group about how it will operate and getting acceptance from those involved, helps to set the tone and create an environment conducive to fairness, participation and, hopefully, trust. The conditions for good group learning cannot be mandated but their significance can be reinforced and modelled by those leading.

We then describe some different approaches to leading a discussion of operating rules and norms to suit different contexts. First, for our three- or four-day intensive workshops, we begin by sharing some rules about how we might behave and treat each other during our time together. They can include, for example:

- Chatham House rules: well-established rules that respect the confidentiality of discussions and state that we as teachers can be quoted but what participants share should not be quoted outside the group.

- Permission to ask questions: encouraging people to contribute, to test the proposition, to relieve the pressure to come to decisions, to just have the discussion and perhaps come back to the way forward after ventilating the ideas.

- Acknowledging differences and the value of hearing different experiences: for example, encouraging those who are quiet to explore their behaviours in a safe environment and those who always ask questions to be thoughtful about their participation. People participate and learn in different ways and we are always amazed at the extraordinary backgrounds and experiences they bring. Sometimes it takes conscious effort to ensure that the value of this diversity is registered in a group setting and that all have the chance to benefit.[6]

- Opportunity for reflection: an invitation to sit back and notice the implicit frameworks, theories and judgements that kick in, what comments by others 'press your buttons' and cause you to react in certain ways. Participants who might normally jump in quickly are encouraged to 'get on the balcony' of both the group and themselves (see chapter 12), to observe the group and their own reactions, and only then consider what might be a useful contribution.

- Willingness to participate: a confirmation that all those involved are volunteers and want to learn from each other and presenters. Very occasionally, people choose to be silent. We reinforce our view that the group is worse off by this silence and misses experience or insights that might otherwise support a better outcome.

- Acknowledging that everyone is equal in the group: no one deserves less or more respect, and there is no reason to defer to others based on their position or perceived importance.

- Suspending judgement and allowing the process to unfold: to be open to new learning and ways of doing things. Our experience has been that the flow of the program is sometimes disconcerting for people, particularly those who come from structured and ordered backgrounds, who might be looking for fast answers. We reinforce that the program is designed to challenge thinking rather than give simplistic answers but that it will support them to come to their own valuable insights.

Depending on the context, the group and the outcomes being sought, and the kinds of principles and values, the process of setting up structure and procedure will vary. Christine has found in her various roles that while the process and set-up were different, it was invaluable to take the time to figure out and establish a clear, well-understood process and in turn a positive, trusting environment. Three examples illustrate this:

1. While Christine was the Police Region Commander on the south coast of New South Wales, she responded to concerns about past habits and introduced a strategy supported by the management team that meetings would be conducted for no longer than two hours; must all have an agenda, ground rules and clear objectives; and, if possible, must be managed by a trained facilitator.

2. Appointed Chief Commissioner of Victoria Police, Christine commenced a series of discussions travelling around the state to get to know many of the members of the organisation and to have them provide input into the challenges and priorities they believed the police were facing. As this was a completely new process in the culture, Christine took care to think about how to introduce, set up and run these meetings. She needed to model openness, listening and a willingness to learn and adapt—the qualities she wanted to encourage within the organisational culture. She says:

   > I began by explaining who I was, talking about my background and family and some of my police experiences. I also told them that I believed I was no better than they were and that I didn't deserve any more or less respect than they did. I wanted to hear from them and would very much value their input so that I could understand the important issues we should concentrate on, to improve the way they were treated and the systems that needed to be fixed. Very

quickly I heard from over six thousand members who trusted me with their concerns. I used a simple technique to write down the issues raised, using a whiteboard and a marker. For those not comfortable speaking openly, a newly established open email system was offered, including the invitation to email me directly—in the past, staff had been forbidden to email the Commissioner.

3. While she was the Victorian Police Commissioner, Christine established a corporate committee to act as the governance body for Victoria Police. With a membership of twenty-six, some people thought this would be unwieldy and time-consuming. But with a clear agenda, good briefing papers, and meetings facilitated by an external trained facilitator, there was improved communication, cross-regional and cross-functional and operational learning, ownership of and commitment to the new directions for change.

The idea of providing a structure and process to support the group to do the work is a principle that both Christine and Amanda have adopted in their leadership work, education and development. It is based on research evidence that, to foster learning and experimentation, and to encourage groups to take responsibility for making changes and adapting to challenges, it is vital that they take ownership of their ways forward. Edicts rarely work in situations that require complex organisational or individual changes.

A second set of examples about the role of leadership in creating space to discuss and establish shared norms comes from Amanda's MBA Leadership and Change classroom. The format is typically a three-hour session each week for ten weeks, which enables us to take more time and foster reflection, and is pivotal to learning new things about leadership and about you as a leader. The first two or three classes involve—via different discussion questions and techniques—opportunities for the group to do the work of identifying and exploring the norms and values by which they want to work together.

The themes that are raised—and often discussed heatedly—include confidentiality, respect and tolerance, opportunities for critique and feedback, safety, personal disclosure, preparedness to be vulnerable, and trust. Inevitably individuals vary in their positions on these issues, partially determined by age, maturity, cultural background and so on. While often individual differences in views and appetites for openness remain, it is the *process* of hearing the concerns of others that enables an understanding of norms to be constructed and creates the basis for trust. For example, while most people begin by wanting a completely 'safe' space for shared discussion, individuals also recognise that risk-taking will be required for new learning. They know that if everyone remains completely comfortable, what unfolds may be predictable and unrewarding. Some individuals will begin to exercise leadership in the group by sharing more openly and being prepared to risk more vulnerability, which in turn builds new norms.

The point we are emphasising is that paying attention to and making space to discuss and establish values and norms is a key but underrated leadership act. Everyone engaged in bringing groups together can exercise this kind of leadership, even if they are located within workplace cultures that operate differently. It may be even more impactful to do so in such environments. There are many ways to invite a discussion and it can be at the start or ongoing, but the process creates possibilities for collaboration, respect and trust, without which no real work will be done.

Partnerships

To be effective—sometimes to survive—leaders need to find partners and allies. Academic researchers and authors, such as Paul 't Hart and Ronald Heifetz, warn against being seduced by the myth of the lone heroic leader.[7] They document that partners are vital, especially in difficult times and in crises, where there is a need for massive mobilisation of effort, and where on-the-run adaption and responsiveness are needed. For example, in their 2009 book *The Practice of Adaptive Leadership*, Heifetz and his co-authors Alexander Grashow and Marty Linsky devote a chapter to the advice 'Don't

Do It Alone'. They identify two common effects when leaders set out on their own to bring about change:

1. their opponents will do whatever it takes to make them vulnerable

2. others opt out or don't take responsibility for their piece of the challenge, thinking 'as long as he or she is willing to go out there and test the ice, good for them'.

Christine emphasises that, whatever their line of work, leaders need partners. Finding and aligning with partners—from inside and outside organisational boundaries, from bosses and staff, from high-profile stakeholders to unlikely allies—has been key to all Christine's roles, and especially those involving significant changes. A partnership can be with one other person or with many in an organisation. Partners give feedback to help you understand the challenges and take heat off you.

It took a while for Amanda—who came to leadership with the rather solitary habits of an academic researcher—to fully appreciate what Christine meant by this. It has also taken her a while to learn how to seek and recognise partners, as well as how to *be* a partner herself. As we described at the start of this chapter, it was Christine's invitation to work alongside her as an observer at Victoria Police that helped Amanda move from being an arm's-length researcher to being an ally and a support in the complexity of leading change.

It is not incidental that our own partnership is between two women. For each of us, working closely with another woman is a very welcome opportunity. As Clementine Ford writes in her book *Fight Like a Girl*, there is a common myth in society that 'women are each other's worst enemies'. Ford argues that this myth has been perpetuated to keep women divided and encourage them to line up alongside and identify with men. She says, 'If women can be convinced to mistrust one another instead of working together, patriarchal order is secured for another day.'[8] We are not disputing that women may encounter female bosses and peers who aren't supportive. But our own experience, including working together and when we work with all-women groups, is that we are stretched and surprised, nourished and enlarged by working in partnership with other women. In our teaching partnerships, if a question or issue stumps one of us we can invite the other to offer a response and this always delivers new insights and examples.

In workshops, Christine says that she can quickly sense who is a partner in the room. By this she means that she can identify the people who are 'with' her, who are interested and engaged, who are open and committed to finding out new things. These people become partners in the leadership learning experience. It is always worth pausing and noticing the other people in the room, those who are silently cheering you on, especially if the work you are doing is difficult or involves challenging the status quo. Identifying partners allows us to recognise we don't carry the burden of change alone and encourages us to avoid martyrdom.

We return to the importance of partnerships later, especially as a support in managing personal and professional risks (see chapter 12), but it is also worth noticing how institutional structures can foster or impede partnerships. When we were writing this book a Royal Commission into Family Violence in Victoria was underway. This followed a harrowing federal inquiry into child sex abuse at the hands of institutions such as the church and schools. In the taking of evidence, the Victorian Commission into Family Violence modelled a partnership by having two or more witnesses together in the witness box. In circumstances where trauma was being investigated, this innovative approach to structure in partnerships helped all the witnesses to have courage and feel supported.

Exploring more

This book is in three parts but, although there is a flow to it that we hope will be compelling, it does not need to be read in order. This chapter and the following, document our case that women have demonstrated leadership and there is much that can be learned from them. Chapter 2 takes a historical perspective, showing how women leaders have been left out of the leadership record. Chapter 3 provides a summary from a wide range of sources and data about the current situation and shows that women leaders still face many subtle and less subtle barriers in fulfilling their potential. These barriers are not from the women or their choices but are persisting features of workplace culture that define leadership in masculine terms, in ways that ensure men are more likely to be seen as 'natural' leadership material.

The second part, 'Achieving', focuses on the bigger picture of leading in organisations. These chapters draw on Christine's extensive leadership experience and the research she has found helpful to identify some lessons—and critique some conventional wisdoms—about how to lead. Chapter 4 focuses on leading change, chapter 5 on leadership in crises, and chapter 6 on strategies for influencing and enabling. In chapter 7 we turn to exploring how to ensure good, effective conversations with those we are seeking to lead. The final chapter of Part 2 suggests that, despite our predominant focus on leadership, good management and managers you would 'walk over hot coals for' are also critical to people being effective and fulfilled in organisations. The content in each of these chapters has been tested with a wide variety of audiences and has proved to be of practical value, whether you are leading an organisation, a team or a community group, or whether you are seeking to mobilise employees, a family, students, activists or volunteers.

Part 3, 'Flourishing', turns the focus on the individual leader and is based on the evidence that good leaders take time to reflect on where they have come from, what they bring, what might hold them back and what they are passionate about helping to shape and change. Chapter 9 explores sources of power and presence that women leaders draw on in their careers and work. In chapter 10, we focus on women leaders' bodies and physicalities. Here we draw particularly on Amanda's research and look at the visibility and scrutiny many women leaders experience, and strategies for responding. Chapter 11 argues that a key to helping leaders flourish is to help them explore changing identities as they navigate stages and transitions in their lives and careers. Chapters 12 and 13, on managing risk and finding resilience and renewal, draw together insights about how to survive with optimism and grace the inevitable setbacks leaders encounter, knowing when to be bold and when to leave. Our final chapter brings together wisdom from women—the women in our programs, senior women who've been panellists and guest speakers, women activists, scholars and authors from the past, and contemporary women writers. These women's words have been helpful and memorable to one or both of us and we hope they will also be so for you.

2
Lessons from the past

Well-behaved women seldom make history.
Professor Laurel Thatcher Ulrich, 2008[1]

In the late 1980s and as a relatively new academic at the University of Melbourne, Amanda was approached by a young woman, Karen Crook, who was interested in doing doctoral research on the Country Women's Association (CWA). The CWA was by far the largest and most well-established women's organisation in Australia, with a long tradition of lobbying successfully for the interests of women and their families. But initially Amanda didn't get it. She recognised that Karen had strong research capabilities and would do excellent work. What she didn't understand was why or how studying the CWA would make an innovative—even radical—contribution in showcasing women's leadership and organising. Amanda initially shared the broader social prejudices of the time, that what women did in organisations like the CWA wasn't leadership and wasn't worth researching and writing about. Karen went on to do an impressive PhD under Amanda's and Professor Patricia Grimshaw's supervision, patiently and powerfully showing that we can learn much from the complexity and dynamism, the battle between conservative and progressive internationalising elements, and the supportive and enabling practices of the CWA.

If we look back at most periods in history, it is not that women have not been leaders but that records have usually been written by men who defined leadership as something that men do. Women's leadership has thus been given other labels, such as 'volunteering', 'community activism' or, more pejoratively, 'trouble-making' and 'meddling'. For example, when Christine was working in Human Resources in the NSW Police, she led and was part of innovative reforms that changed the culture of policing. However, they often went unrecognised because it was women who led them.

Other examples of women's leadership contributions being left out came to light during Hillary Clinton's bid for the US presidency. Commentators remind us that the leadership of many women presidents and prime ministers has often been overlooked, including that of American woman Janet Rosenberg, who was the first president of Guyana.[2] Fifty-four countries have had female presidents or prime ministers in recent history, many of whom introduced progressive changes to their countries. With a few exceptions, their contribution as leaders has been ignored, and their ascendancy put down to family connections rather than their own leadership capabilities. Women have also been reluctant to claim credit for the contribution their leadership might have made. Historic and contemporary examples show that when women put themselves out there and draw attention to their aims, activities and successes, they are often targeted for extra criticism or attack, as we explore further in Part 3.

Stories of women's leadership from the past have inspired us in our work and life, but their stories have often been confined to the margins of official 'his-tory' or, worse, not told. As former Australian Governor-General Quentin Bryce describes in her 2013 Boyer Lectures, women sharing stories—their own and those of their mothers, grandmothers and other female forebears—is a way to change attitudes, to assuage fear and promote healing, to connect and hold societies accountable. We believe there is much to be learned from how women have led in the past despite often overwhelming societal obstacles, social stereotypes and discrimination, and a lack of financial and political rights. From these stories, we want to encourage women to be brave about what they are seeking to do, to have confidence to tell their stories, to claim their leadership and the leadership contribution of other women.

Learning from women leaders in history

Writing women's leadership back into historical accounts is an endeavour that has steadily gained momentum. They are rich and instructive examples of leadership because they have often been undertaken against the tide of social norms and have required courage, perseverance and resilience. We also suggest here the importance of monitoring how leadership stories are told. The question needs to be persistently asked: Where are women doing crucial leadership work that doesn't get noticed or recorded because it doesn't look like a tough, heroic performance?

An example of how history has neglected women's leadership is revealed in historian Clare Wright's award-winning 2013 book, *The Forgotten Rebels of Eureka*. When she read histories of the 1854 Eureka uprising—often regarded as the birthplace of Australian democracy—she wondered whether women were even *at* the goldfields. Her primary research—going back to original documents—showed they were not just there but were propelling the very course of events, as journalists, activists, community leaders and business operators. It turns out that women were a third of the population on Victorian goldfields in the mid nineteenth century as the environment was potentially a liberating, if challenging, one for women. With a loosening of social structures and the men busy mining, women ran shops and businesses and were also miners and often family breadwinners. Wright argues that putting women back into the story of Eureka actually *changes* the story, moving them from bystander roles, like sewing the famous flag, to leadership roles. The local newspaper editor was a woman and she used her paper to campaign against extortionate fines. Another woman was a poet and writer whose published letters became the voice of the community. While the roles of male rebels at the barricades have been romanticised, in Wright's view it was often the women who provided leadership by articulating issues, organising and mobilising.

Women's organisations have been pivotal in Australia across a wide range of contexts and issues, from creating family-based services through to policing. In the 1890s, the National Council of Women (NCW) began advocating for women to be part of the police force. Initially they were to police women, but later the NCW and their history of effort became a crucial support for Christine working in the NSW Police, making the case for women to be in all policing roles and to put more focus on ensuring women's safety.

A source of valuable documentation of Australian women's leadership in history is a large research project of which Amanda was a part, led by historians from Melbourne University and other universities, including Joy Damousi, Patricia Grimshaw and Rosemary Francis.[3] A range of case studies and historical analyses reveals extensive leadership by Australian women over a century of emerging democracy in politics, science and the professions, in the media, community, Indigenous affairs and elsewhere. This was often against intractable institutional obstacles and some men in positions of formal leadership determined to keep those women silent and powerless.[4] Among the lessons we wish to convey here is the importance of not just taking the time to understand the obstacles women have faced but recognising—and learning from—the spirit, the audacity, the creativity and the subversiveness by which they changed societies. Don't miss seeing this leadership just because institutional authorities and academics haven't given it that label, or because the women involved didn't blow their own trumpet about it.

Further afield, international women's movements of all kinds provide powerful examples of change being led by women. Women's leadership has often had to be devolved and shared at local and community levels because there was no other way to access power and get decision-makers to take notice.[5] Radical and disruptive tactics have sometimes been part of these leadership approaches, as was the case with the English suffragette movement. As graphically portrayed in the film *Suffragette*, the women urged on by the Pankhursts tried working through recognised mechanisms and political channels. When these failed, they were forced to hold public demonstrations, which led to prison for some, and hunger strikes. Pioneering Australian women activists fighting for equal pay, such as Zelda D'Aprano, followed suffragette tactics. Zelda chained herself to government offices to get attention to the cause and was successful, after trying for many years, to get change through formal channels of union and government.

Another example of suffragette tactics—also from the early twentieth century—is described by American feminist Gloria Steinem, who visited India in the 1950s.[6] Interviewing Kamaladevi Chattopadhyay, a rare woman leader in the Indian independence struggle, Steinem was extolling the virtues of Gandhi's approach to working at the local level. Chattopadhyay respectfully pointed out that much of Gandhi's leadership was modelled on what he had seen in the suffragette movement in London and, before that, the massive Indian social movement led by women against suttee, the practice of burning widows with their husbands.

Women organising

From the late 1960s onwards, internationally various women's movements coincided and collaborated with environmental, community and human rights activism. Women were often key leaders in these movements and formed themselves into organisations to lobby more effectively and to have their voices heard. In Australia, these included politically oriented groups such as the Women's Electoral Lobby (created to improve the numbers of women successfully elected to all levels of government) and EMILY's List (an Australian off-shoot of the American organisation, led by former Victorian Premier Joan Kirner among others and that aims to help elect women candidates), as well as grass-roots, national and international organisations.

As Amanda elaborates in chapter 11 when she describes the emergence of her interest in women's leadership and feminism, it wasn't until she started to research women in local government—or more accurately the lack of them at that time—that she started to understand the extent of women's leadership and the challenges they were facing. Groups like the Australian Local Government Women's Association and the Women's Electoral Lobby were organised and have been effective in supporting often-lone women to take on elected roles where there was routine harassment, disparagement and sometimes sabotage from some fellow councillors who were intent on keeping the status quo.[7]

Through the 1970s and 1980s there was also extensive activism in federal and state bureaucracies in Australia, where women worked as ministers and bureaucrats to improve opportunities for women. This activity included the introduction of various forms of anti-discrimination legislation in the 1970s and the *Affirmative Action (Equal Employment for Women) Act 1986*. Seen as global leaders in women's policy initiatives, a substantial cadre of women bureaucrats, sometimes referred to as femocrats, in this country led reform initiatives within bureaucracies.[8] Women's advisers were appointed to the prime minister in the mid 1970s. In state government, offices for women's affairs were created, such as the Women's Co-ordination Unit in New South Wales. For Christine, working within the NSW Government, these offices and the women working in them were vital as advocates for legislative and other reforms to improve women's equality and safety but, more particularly, strong supporters and partners in the changes she was seeking; for example, introducing maternity leave in policing and tackling issues such as sexual assault and family violence.

Federal- and state-based equal opportunity legislation required bureaucracies and large companies to keep data on the number of women selected and promoted and to run programs designed to improve awareness of the benefits of diversity. These measures and institutional initiatives resulted in networks of senior women leaders, academics and equal opportunity practitioners working for reform and innovation in the public sector and corporate spheres. The relatively large number of women in senior roles in state and federal governments, and increasingly in local governments, is one result of this combined work during the 1980s and 1990s.

Indigenous traditions of women's leadership

The leadership of indigenous women around the world against traditional, patriarchal and colonial authorities has only recently begun to be recognised and recorded. In her memoir, feminist Gloria Steinem writes about being invited to join 'talking circles' in many cultural and global contexts where women have had few other opportunities to voice their situations. Such circles are an ancient form of governance, widely used in indigenous societies and often supplanted with hierarchical structures as part of colonisation. The leadership principles espoused within the talking circles are:

- If you want people to listen to you, you have to listen to them.

- If you hope people will change how they live, you have to know how they live.

- If you want people to see you, you have to sit down with them eye to eye.[9]

Among the most moving accounts of women's leadership are from Australia's Indigenous women leaders.[10] Scholars are increasingly documenting the ways Indigenous women have enacted leadership in the face of the deliberate dehumanising sexism and racism that accompanied colonisation and continues today.[11] Usually without formal positions, grandmothers, aunties and female elders have provided leadership through recording cultural practices and elder wisdom, teaching and mentoring in culture and art and poetry to keep fragile cultures alive.[12] Experiencing the simultaneous oppressions of racism and sexism, women have often been the leadership brokers between worlds by being advocate, spokesperson and recorder of cultural and community values as well as change agent, charged with making adaptations in the face of the erosion of traditional values by Western norms. Research shows it has been women leaders who have often developed culturally derived models of governance to work together to achieve good community outcomes, and to uphold their cultures through story, art and song, while engaging across Australian and international political and human rights networks.[13]

Academic Jackie Huggins has documented her experience of leadership and of how she benefited from the models of other Aboriginal women leaders such as Evelyn Scott, Lowitja O'Donoghue and Doris Pilkington. Huggins says that for her, 'Leadership means that you need to respect differences of views and start where people are at—not where you want them to be. The trick is listen, listen, listen, then act.' She goes on to elaborate some of the features of the way Indigenous women lead, in her experience, including:

- having the interests of community at heart, putting care of community at the centre of one's work

- being prepared to step up and take responsibility, which creates a 'chain reaction' in mentoring young people in a 'culturally appropriate' transfer of roles

- 'never forgetting where you've come from or who put you there'

- being honest, respecting other people and yourself, being clear about what you can do and what you can't, admitting if you don't know

- knowing your strength but also accepting help and acknowledging support (especially from aunties)—leadership is never done alone

- trusting instinct and gut reactions

- in her own case Huggins says she connects to her mother who died some years ago, feeling her 'tap on my shoulder' and calling in the ancestors encouraging her to 'go for it' and urging her sisters to do so too.[14]

Huggins' emphases encapsulate the features we often see that distinguish women's leadership. These include the importance placed on leading in a collaborative, consultative way, of mentoring and caring across generational lines, of the spiritual, embodied and instinctual in leadership.[15]

Have there been women's ways of leading?

Reappraising the rewritten historical record, it is abundantly clear that women have provided leadership over centuries.[16] However, they have largely not done so at the head of institutions or governments. Rather, women have been notable leaders in unions and workplace rights, and in community, consumer and environmental movements. They have led in philanthropy and emerging professions, such as social work. Women in areas such as science have often had to change institutions and countries or join and hold office in international networks to get recognition for their work and leadership. Women have specialised particularly in using writing and stories to raise consciousness, for example about Indigenous history and culture.

Although it is controversial to argue that there is a female way of leading, what emerges from research are several lessons about the way women have changed societies, usually from the margins, often while juggling family responsibilities and without formal power. Some of the features of the leadership of women in history include:

- When seeing situations of inequity, prejudice and suffering, women have spoken out and stood up against contemporary opinion and conventionally accepted practices, for example in their pioneering role as factory inspectors.

- Women have advocated and demonstrated how locally developed and governed initiatives are more likely to be accepted and implemented, as with the case of 1970s activism in communities, reform of local government and in indigenous communities.

- Eschewing charismatic leadership from the front along with the role of 'leader', women have often emphasised and argued for the value of shared leadership, of consensus building as well as achieving goals, and of the value, *in itself*, of supporting and nurturing group members and valuing participation and community development. These kinds of leadership have been particularly evident in the arts, in migrant and refugee communities, and in parts of the environmental movement.

- Individual women are noteworthy because they have generally not allowed themselves or their activism to be constrained by wanting to be liked or approved of, wanting to be 'one of the boys'. As extensive research has shown, for example in corporate governance, homogeneity in the form of 'hegemonic masculinity' acts as a powerful pull towards 'group-think' or seeking concurrence of opinions. Men in all-male or homogeneous groups do not want to speak up or depart from group opinion for fear of looking stupid.[17] Many of the causes of corporate disasters and scandals can be traced to senior board members or executives failing to speak up about their concerns for these reasons. In contrast, women are often already in the position of outsider and so have less to lose from going against group opinion.

- Working in communities and groups, women leaders have often demonstrated openness and a desire to promote diversity in the people they work alongside or lead.[18] Women have often found natural allies among other outsiders or those who have experienced oppression. Women have also banded together, acknowledging their diversity but working towards an overarching agenda, for example initiatives undertaken by the National Council of Women that accommodated both conservative and progressive women's groups.

- Women have been strategic, for example forging international alliances, to bring momentum and visibility to a need for change.

- Reading historical accounts shows women mixing courage with a refreshing practicality and an ability to see and use the opportunities at hand to influence, rather than wait to mobilise change through or from formal positions of authority

Telling stories of women's leadership

One of the things you notice when looking at leadership is that it is usually a story of men. Men are the heroes of leadership and entrepreneurial biographies. Most of the case studies profile men achieving, whether in sport, exploration, science, the arts, business or any other field of endeavour. In areas of business and management, the 'brand leaders' and entrepreneurs held up as exemplars are almost universally men, despite women being a very significant proportion of business creators. This is not because women haven't been leading, but that what they have been doing hasn't been recorded, or hasn't been recorded as leadership. Our desire is to encourage people to ask how the leadership story is told, in particular how women are sidelined. If you are tempted to think this is just a historical problem, it is worth homing in on contemporary accounts of leadership. In the 'Leadership of the National Disability Insurance Scheme' box, we provide one example of how public commentary and learning about leadership continues to focus on high-profile men rather than on women and communities in getting big changes to happen.

One of the obstacles to women's leadership stories being recognised has been men's control of the media as owners and editors, and in academia as gatekeepers of research. With what could be seen as a democratisation of media through social media, women journalists, bloggers and researchers have found new ways to document women's experiences and to organise and support each other across international borders, especially with those who are disenfranchised and silenced within traditional structures.[19] This level of research and writing, bringing with it activism and collaboration, has created what some see as fourth-wave feminism, or a new, re-energised feminism that is less concerned about academic categories and more interested in changing societies to end the subordination of women. These opinion leaders and agitators are providing new forms of leadership for women and for societies more broadly.

NDIS: How the leadership story has been told

The introduction of the Australian National Disability Insurance Scheme (NDIS) by the Australian parliament in 2012 is recognised as a landmark achievement. By 2022 it will enable over half a million people to access comprehensive disability and caring services. Costing in the order of $25 billion, the scheme received bipartisan support and unprecedented community support, and was viewed widely as reform overdue in a sector at breaking point.

How has the leadership of this legislative and policy innovation been told? In many popular accounts, men feature as leaders, especially then MInister for Workplace Relations Bill Shorten, and previous Health Minister Brian Howe. Our purpose citing this case is not to reduce men's roles but to show that women and communities provided vital leadership in the NDIS that should not be overlooked.

In a series of podcasts by *The Conversation* entitled 'Change Agents', one program was dedicated to discussing the introduction of the NDIS.[20] The two panellists interviewed were Rhonda Galbally and Bruce Bonyhady, both inaugural members (Bonyhady was Chair) of the NDIS Advisory Group (a new Board was appointed in late 2016, on which Galbally sits as well as chairing the Advisory Council). The podcast relates the role of high-profile male leaders and the institutional struggles between organisations in the disability sector to get the scheme up and running. When Galbally is brought into the discussion she moves the focus in quite a different direction.

Rhonda Galbally has been a leader in the areas of health, disability and community activism since the early 1980s. A CEO of five new organisations, including the Victorian Health Promotion Foundation (VicHealth) (1988–98) and Our Community, an organisation she co-founded (2000–10), Rhonda acquired polio as a child and has had limited mobility since. She has been, by any measure, a pioneering leader in areas of public and women's health, and disability.

In the podcast, she stresses how community activism was key in the birth of the NDIS, for example how 'disability teas' were held in organisations around Australia, and how a massive campaign was mobilised with 120 members of federal parliament visited by someone with a disability. She highlighted the importance of getting all the stakeholders together, including carers' organisations. She knew from personal experience how important carers were, recalling the struggles and isolation of her own mother caring for a young child with polio. Rhonda also drew attention to the key roles of female politicians, including then Prime Minister Julia Gillard and Minister Jenny Macklin, who had commissioned data collection and research to explore how to fund the scheme and who successfully took the proposal to the Senate Estimates Committee for approval.

Rhonda also recalls her personal contact with Tony Abbott, then Leader of the Opposition, who was expected to be a stumbling block in the NDIS: 'I bumped into Tony Abbott in the street in Sydney and said "I am so pleased to hear you are supporting the NDIS." He said, "In most cases I'm Mr No. In this case, I'm Mr Yes."' Galbally quoted his response in her subsequent National Press Club address. Abbott began quoting it too. The incident conveys something of Rhonda's leadership: her direct, personal appeal to someone seen as a stumbling block.

In this NDIS example, as in many others, we need to ensure that the leadership story is not just one focusing on the individual actions of men or the big decisions of institutions. In listening to Galbally's experiences and commentary, we hear another leadership story. In this version leadership has been provided by individuals living with disabilities who were prepared to tell their stories, by carers who got involved and lobbied parliamentarians, by the activism of small groups, organisations and communities who raised awareness and educated broadly, by women politicians prepared to do the backroom work to resolve funding and administrative hurdles, and by many apparently small conversations initiated by people like Rhonda who were prepared to invite the support of those who might otherwise be sceptics or bystanders. It is these conversations and activities that must be considered leadership. Just as much as the speeches in parliament, it was this mobilisation that got the NDIS over the line.

3
Where women are now

> *One of the most comfortable things about assumptions* [that women aren't suited to leadership] *is they don't feel like assumptions at all. Mostly, they just feel like the natural way of things.*
>
> Annabel Crabb, 2014

The data about the current representation of women in leadership, and especially in business and management leadership roles, shows that progress in creating opportunities for women to assume senior executive roles in organisations has stalled. Any way you look at it, in all parts of the world, the area of organisational leadership remains stubbornly the domain of men. This, we argue, is not a problem of women or their talent or abilities, it is a failure of leadership.

Our intent in summarising contemporary data in this chapter is to help women stay clear-eyed and focused on their path in leadership. We want women to be prepared for the kinds of obstacles they may face—and many young women may not face any obstacles until they plan to start a family or rise to more senior roles where they are directly competing with men who may earlier have been their mentors. We also want women to feel empowered in their leadership not to conform to models that don't feel right for them or that require them to turn themselves into someone different to succeed. Our view is that too often, in both the popular and academic literature, the focus has been on giving women tips to lean in to a culture of leadership that itself should be problematised.[1] By understanding the current situation, our hope is that women leaders will challenge and change leadership.

Paths to leadership

Data from Australia and internationally show that women are now completing undergraduate and graduate degrees in equivalent or greater numbers than men (66 per cent of Australian graduates are women). Women earn more than 50 per cent of PhDs in many areas, including some parts of the sciences, economics and business. They are also likely to be strongly represented (half of intakes) at organisational entry levels in many industries and sectors, such as law, accounting and medicine and even traditionally very male-dominated environments like engineering and science. Women are well represented in entrepreneurial and small business roles, in parts of the arts and media sectors. However, as they seek executive and leadership roles in large organisations, numbers of women drop off dramatically and are replaced by men in senior management.

In Australia women are about 45 per cent of middle managers, 10 per cent of executives and 2 to 3 per cent of CEOs. At the most senior levels of management, men are nine times more likely to achieve C-suite positions, such as chief executive officer (CEO), chief operating officer (COO) or chief financial officer (CFO), than women. In all parts of the world and across sectors, women typically represent just 3 to 4 per cent of CEOs. The dramatic contrast between the distribution of men and women at entry versus the most senior levels of Australian companies has been captured in a report by Bain & Company and Chief Executive Women.[2]

In the 2016 report of the Australian Workplace Gender Equality Agency, proactive actions by, for example, the Australian Stock Exchange and Australian Institute of Company Directors have seen the proportion of women board directors increased to 25 per cent. However, the number of women chairs has gone down.[3] Analysis provides no confidence that the proportion of women in these roles will continue to rise.

Explanations commonly invoked in business contexts for the continuing absence—or exclusion—of women in senior management roles are women's opting at peak-career times to scale back due to family responsibilities, women's absence of line management experience and reluctance to be mobile, women's lack of mentoring and exclusion from networks, and how women's leadership styles are seen and evaluated. While all these explanations have been well rehearsed—and researched—our argument is that much of the discussion about obstacles to women in leadership has left out key issues such as power and identities. Arguments for encouraging women into leadership have often been couched in 'the business case', as if laying out the rational, commercial evidence about hiring, retaining and promoting women will shift mindsets.

Decisions about leaders and leadership are rarely based on transparent, rational calculations of merit. As women move higher up in organisations they are competing with men for increasingly scarce power, resources and opportunities. Decisions about who to appoint into leadership roles are more likely to be informed by the judgements of peers around 'fit' or 'look', or the legitimacy of previous leadership experience that is 'not quite the CEO experience' boards and headhunters say they are looking for—which many men invited onto boards also don't have. It is systemic, attitudinal factors that prevent women from taking their place in leadership.

Theories for women's absence/exclusion from leadership

Among the most common theories for why the drop-off of women occurs at the leadership level is that early professional and managerial career building coincides with child bearing and rearing. Indeed, women's workforce participation drops off at this time of their life. But there are two problems with attributing the low numbers of women in leadership to the fact that women have children and typically (though not always) take responsibility for looking after them in the very early years.

The first, though not to put too much emphasis on work–family conflicts as the explanation for women's absence, is that research demonstrates there are a significant proportion of women who don't have children or who take minimum time out from their careers to have them.[4] Women are no less ambitious than their male colleagues even though women also want to have children.[5] The second, related reason, also shown in research is that it is organisational conditions and pressures that make it difficult for women to gain promotion, not women's decision to have children.

The main obstacle women face is the one in the minds of the headhunters, selection panels and boards that second-guess when women might fall pregnant or think they won't want to take a promotion that involves moving. With these mindsets, they then fail to appoint women to leadership roles. It is not the women who are making these decisions. What has been termed the 'motherhood penalty' exists, with one in five women experiencing discrimination around the time they become or might become parents. For example, even though it is against the law, evidence indicates that decision-makers routinely act on assumptions about women and their plans and ambitions that are not considered when it comes to men. Women are therefore excluded from promotion pools or subtly dropped down the list of eligible candidates. Or employers make it very difficult for women to return after maternity leave at an equivalent managerial level or in a part-time capacity. It is organisational cultures and conditions that are the problem, not women's biology or their desire to have children.[6]

These factors were studied in an aptly titled longitudinal study of over five thousand American women engineering graduates, 'Leaning In But Getting Pushed Back (and Out)' by psychological researcher Nadya Fouad. It showed that only a small proportion of women leave engineering management to pursue caregiving and family responsibilities.[7] Of equal importance in their decision to leave their companies and/or engineering was that women were not offered opportunities for advancement. Over 68 per cent of women who had left were working in managerial roles outside engineering, not sitting at home knitting or baking cakes for fundraising drives—though there is nothing wrong with doing so! Of those who left the profession five or fewer years previously, two-thirds left to pursue better opportunities elsewhere. One-third said they had left to assume family responsibilities because their employers were not flexible enough to accommodate work–life balance.

A compounding and clearly demonstrated factor working against women pursuing leadership is inequitable pay. The pay gap for equal work has increased, not decreased, in Australia. In 2004 it was around 15 per cent. The Workplace for Gender Equality 2016 report found that women were paid 17 per cent less across all industries but the discrepancy was higher in some industries, such as retail. At the top-most level, men earned $93,800 more than women. In some senior roles in the law and among executives, the difference between what equally qualified and able men and women get paid can be as high as 28 per cent. This pay gap is already in play at graduate entry levels and it also has increased, not reduced, from 3.8 per cent in 2011 to 9.3 per cent in 2012.[8]

Why does this gap exist and why has it increased not lessened? Increasingly, pay is up for negotiation and studies show men are more likely to successfully negotiate higher pay. Yet the solution is not to just teach and advocate for women to negotiate harder, because research also shows that women who are tough negotiators are judged more harshly, seen as unduly aggressive and ambitious, and are not necessarily rewarded. What we may see in these statistics is a vicious circle where women are valued less and paid less for equivalent work, and even when they reach the top of their organisations and careers, their leadership is still seen as worth less in dollar terms than that of their male counterparts.

Most explanations for the absence of women in leadership positions continue to focus on what women should do, including that women need to:

- stick with their careers even when things get very tough, including delaying starting a family to fit around career or choosing to forgo one

- be more ambitious and make their case for promotion, not reproduce socialised patterns of not taking credit for their achievements[9]

- shed their attachment to being, to use journalist Annabel Crabb's phrase, 'super-competent'[10]

- get better at saying 'no', at getting help at home and negotiating harder to share responsibilities with partners

- seek more line management experience with responsibility for bigger budgets, and not allow themselves to be sidelined in Human Resources, Corporate Affairs or other non-line roles

- be offered special mentoring or sponsorship, because they are not part of the informal networks and the informal job market.

While many of these remedies may seem sensible and much effort continues to be put into them, the evidence is that they don't have much effect right at the top—at leadership levels. From our point of view many of these remedies are focused on the wrong thing. Many initiatives assume a 'deficit' model, where women need help to overcome their deficiencies, their lack of 'fit' for leadership. Research has consistently and clearly demonstrated that most of these efforts don't work. They are focused on getting a few, isolated and outstanding women over the hurdles to leadership but they don't usher in lasting change in leadership cultures.

It is only by understanding and changing the ways leadership is defined, and the norms by which it is measured, that we will see sustainable change in the diversity and inclusiveness of leadership cultures. So, as well as asking where women are at in leadership, we also want to ask where the leadership culture is at.

Where the leadership culture is now

Journalist and author Catherine Fox identifies some of the assumptions that are still part of mainstream thinking about leadership and women in her book *Seven Myths about Women and Work*.[11] These are:

- the workforce is a meritocracy

- the gender pay gap is exaggerated

- mothers lack ambition

- women need to act more like men

- targets and quotas are unnecessary

- there are not enough interested women to achieve equality

- time will heal all or 'the pipeline' will eventually deliver.

Working through each assumption, Fox provides detailed evidence to show how each is unfounded yet still governs decision-making in organisations and in leadership.

In her book *The Wife Drought*, commentator Annabel Crabb deftly captures the absurdity of rigid gender roles and their dark consequences. She shows that women are held back from leadership by societal assumptions and norms. These are taken-for-granted ideas about work, gender and who looks 'normal' in top-paying leadership jobs. These norms are very powerful and families who depart from them come under intense pressure to conform to the 'woman at home and in part-time work / man as the main breadwinner and working long hours' model. The assumptions include:

- it is inappropriate for men who are serious about their career and leadership to take extended time out from work and career to assist in child rearing or elder care

- women should do the bulk of household and family duties, even those in full-time employment and those who earn more than their partner—indeed, Crabb documents an alarming U-curve where women earning significantly more than their partner are likely to spend more time on family and domestic responsibilities, not less

- it is more 'natural' for men to be the main breadwinners and women—around the world, it turns out—go to great lengths to shield their partners' sensibilities about money and career, preferring instead to preserve the relationship

- women are better or more 'naturally suited' to bringing up children

- men need and deserve to be paid more

- men with families are leadership material, while women with families in leadership are suspect—they either are neglecting their families or are not real women because they've chosen not to have children.[12]

In the case of each of these assumptions and sets of norms, Crabb assembles solid international research and an absurdist turn of phrase to show how misplaced they are. For example, on the assumption that women are better at bringing up children, she draws on Norwegian and other research showing that everyone—child, mother and father—benefits from parenting being shared much more equally. The myth that fathers can't do it is unfounded and the decision about who takes the predominant role in child rearing is more likely to be due to social norms, calculations on lost earnings and protecting male egos and career continuity. In the case of public life, men are rewarded for having families—it's a mark of their dependability—while senior women are in a no-win situation of constantly being judged as either not having 'enough love in them' to have children, or being too greedy in wanting to 'have it all' if they do.

These contemporary analyses reflect similar conclusions to those Amanda reached in her work with colleagues on Australian leadership culture in the 1990s and reported in *Trials at the Top* in 1994 and *Doing Leadership Differently* in 1998. Ascending to and occupying a leadership role in an organisation or public sphere is judged—and supported or not—within a cultural context. Who gets to the top and is recognised as 'leadership material' is determined and supported by cultural myths, stereotypes and social norms, not by rational argument or calculations of merit and ability. Efforts to maintain power and shore up an acceptable identity are a central part of what's going on. We will not make progress if we ignore these dynamics or pretend that change is simply a matter of allowing rational evidence to take its course.

What about 'the business case' for gender diversity?

The business case for diversity aims to show a clear financial and performance benefit to organisations from employing diverse employees. There is increasingly extensive data demonstrating that diversity is potentially good for employees and for business—measured in various ways. These benefits are not realised, though, by simply recruiting diverse employees and putting them together. It's not a simple input–output calculation. Organisations need to implement policies and strategies to ensure the potential benefits of diversity are realised.[13]

Indeed, we believe this thinking is part of the problem. Relying on the business case to justify making organisations more inclusive is flawed in itself. It locks researchers and human resource directors into tirelessly trying to finally and unequivocally demonstrate diversity's benefits. As some have noted, men don't have to justify their financial value as board members and rarely are senior male executives required to show their 'add' to the bottom line. Converting the issue into one of profit and financial gain delegitimises arguments of fairness, justice, ethics and equality of opportunity.[14] Even with the evidence of the business case, many organisations keep recruiting only men into senior executive roles. Continuing to rely on the economic arguments for employing women in leadership appears not to produce significant change.

Remedying the problem of women's exclusion from leadership and the loss of their talent in organisations may require more radical measures, such as governments setting quotas for the proportion of women on boards, or, less controversially, organisations establishing 'targets with teeth'; that is, targets that have financial and other measurable performance penalties and incentives attached.[15] Under targets with teeth, if executives don't meet their targets of selection, promotion and retention of women then the performance rating of those executives suffers, with flow-on effects to their promotional prospects, bonuses and so on. In their extensive review of international research, policy and practice, Jennifer Whelan and Robert Wood recommend that targets should be linked to performance and to 'at-risk/variable remuneration'.[16] In addition, while quotas have been controversial they have been used successfully in overseas corporate and political contexts—for example, in political parties requiring a certain proportion of women pre-selected to winnable seats.[17]

Why improve the representation of women in leadership?

There are many reasons why we should work towards improving the representation of women in leadership, and those reasons may seem so obvious as to not needing to be restated here. However, it is important to emphasise equality and justice arguments, and arguments about improving the quality and impact of leadership, as well as the more common economic or 'human capital' arguments. The first category of reasons are that women have a right to be treated equally without discrimination or prejudice. We live in societies that pride themselves on being meritocratic, where every child, whatever their gender, can expect opportunities to fulfil their potential.

The second category of reasons deals with leadership. Although widely studied, there is a lot of evidence to indicate that much of the leadership offered in today's organisations and communities is flawed—occasionally corrupt but more often ineffective, unskilful, lacking vision and hope. There is plenty of room for improvement in the field of leadership. Organisational cultures that have been dominated by men, such as the military, police and firefighting, often develop norms around the performance of leadership that advance narrow definitions of social goals and are not open to innovation. High degrees of homogeneity in groups has been linked with a lack of transparency and accountability, with bullying and harassment, for example in the military, and sometimes with authoritarianism, the misuse or abuse of power, for example among peacekeeping organisations.

In a further example, researchers into the devastating 2009 Victorian bushfires argue that women's leadership *should* be valued and that traditional responses to fire were sometimes governed by misplaced notions of heroic leadership. They found consistent evidence that some men felt bound to stay and defend their home, believing that this notion of heroic implacability was what was required of them. There was also evidence of many disagreements between spouses, with men much more likely to argue for families staying and defending homes while their wives advocated following advice, packing up and leaving. Despite the tragic consequences of the decision to stay and fight a fire, researcher Meagan Tyler noted that, still, men's behaviour in defending their property continued to be lionised as heroic while women wanting to evacuate were cast in the media as passive or weak.[18] In this example, as in others, habitual models and norms of leadership must be questioned, and looking to the way some women lead is likely to provide positive alternative role models.

Sometimes the argument is made that improving the representation of women and women with power will have flow-on effects to wider social goals, such as reducing sexism and the incidence of domestic violence. It makes sense that this might be the case, that increasing women's visibility in leadership will reduce stereotyping and increase the respect with which women are treated. However, there are good reasons not to pin the case for putting women into leadership on the expectation that they will—individually or collectively—bring a 'civilising' influence.[19] This expectation puts an additional burden on women and can solidify stereotypes and unhelpful dichotomies—for example, leaving women to do the emotional, caring work of leadership while men are relieved of the need to worry about the 'human side'. Rather, we should be advocating for women in leadership to ensure all people have opportunities to contribute and realise their potential. The quality of leadership and aspiring future leaders will also benefit from more diverse models and exemplars.

The argument about whether women do leadership differently has been widely canvassed. There is some evidence that, when able to develop their own structures and goals, women do organise themselves and lead differently. Certainly, our experience working with all-women groups is that women together are usually very generous in the learning and support they provide for one another. Yet it is also important to recognise the diversity in the way women organise and lead. We join with other researchers keen to shine a light on, and learn from, the many ways women have mobilised their communities, improved opportunities, inspired, and been role models for others coming behind them.

How to improve opportunities for women in leadership

Too often, when challenged to change leadership, the response is to 'fix the women'. Instead, we want to emphasise the practical actions men can take, the interventions that change systems, and some actions that women can take. When Christine has addressed audiences, and especially audiences dominated by men, she suggests the following practical actions that help people take responsibility for change and be part of the solution.

What men can do
- Stop using your power to undermine, harm, manipulate, dominate, bully and reinforce gender norms and sexism.

- Use your power and social capital to fix the situation for women.

- Think about the bias to 'think manager, think male', and stop appointing people who look like you.

- Remember daughters, nieces, sisters and female friends and realise that other men who stereotype and choose individuals who look like themselves will damage these women's futures, preventing them accessing jobs and opportunities they are entitled to.

- Male partners, husbands, fathers, brothers, family members, neighbours, bosses and colleagues need to step up and make it a level playing field for all women and girls.

- Value women's perspectives in business—our communities will be richer for them.

Strategies to change systems

- Pay women the same as men for the same jobs. It's not hard.

- Construct a bias-free appointment/promotion system.

- Implement flexible work conditions and a policy of asking, 'If this work can't be done part time, why not?'

- Provide for paternity and maternity leave, and carer support.

- Reveal unconscious bias and train others to see how it reduces equal opportunity,

- Use external/independent people in selection processes and where possible 'blind' panels, where the gender of the applicant is removed or not known.

- Recognise that companies are more profitable with women on their boards and in leadership.

- Track the costs and investment lost when women leave for lack of a flexible workplace.

- Layer different kinds of strategies and interventions to build up concerted effect.

Actions women can undertake

- Don't wait for time to heal the issues—argue for targets and quotas.

- Put up your hand, take your seat at the table, find your voice.

- Stop being afraid.

- Don't act like men: it's a waste of a good woman.

- Don't believe that all the work has been done—the research shows it hasn't.

- Many gender differences are the result of socialisation—they are not the truth about men or women and they can be undone and changed.

- Keep a scorecard of your experience.

- Give a hand up to other women.

Part 2

ACHIEVING

We now shift from a general focus on women leading to the practical: what women can do in their leadership work to achieve valuable outcomes and organisational change. The following five chapters include a distillation of experience, particularly Christine's, in various leadership roles, as well as management, organisational and leadership research, to provide ideas and insights about how to achieve change. These chapters are addressed to anyone involved in leadership. It is not just for those with formal leadership and management roles. It is for everyone seeking to influence others towards good outcomes.

4
Twelve lessons in leading change

> *If you want people to follow you in a new direction, you must invite them along. You must be clear about where they are going, and you must explain why your route there is superior to the one they are accustomed to taking.*
>
> Christine Nixon, 2011

History shows that women are well positioned to lead institutional change. Women often have less of an interest in maintaining the status quo than men who've worked their way to the top and are comfortable with the way things are. Women are also often experienced in ushering in changes using skills of inspiration, persuasion and negotiation, without the benefit of formal authority or position.

A key theme of Christine's career has been about introducing changes. These include programs designed to improve the numbers and the range of work opportunities for women in policing, from the 1970s till now. They include the introduction of the Safety House Program in New South Wales, community policing and improved responses to sexual assault and child abuse, alongside organisational innovations involving work systems, human resources and structural reforms. In her two roles, as Police Commissioner and as Chair of the Bushfire Reconstruction and Recovery Authority, change—wanted or not—has been at the heart of her leadership. Her subsequent roles, including as Chair of Good Shepherd Microfinance, as a Council member and then Deputy Chancellor of Monash University and Chair of Monash College, have also involved leading or being part of changes in the tertiary education and not-for-profit sectors and have involved shifting the mindset of employees, managers and the community about what is possible and about how to increase positive impacts in defined social and economic goals.

Arising from these experiences Christine has identified twelve lessons that have been fundamental to her approach and can guide the successful implementation of change.[1] The emphases in Christine's lessons are very different from those in most other books on leading change, and include a pre-eminent focus on respecting and caring for the people you are seeking to lead. Reflecting her experiences as a woman leader, her advice offers a distinctive but powerful set of insights about processes of achieving important outcomes in leadership. Interwoven in these lessons are both research and examples.

1   Respect those you lead

The first important lesson I learned as a police officer was to take account of and respect the people who were working with and, later, for me in the organisation. In the 1980s I was young and was seen by some as a bit of a smart-arse. I was trying to convince senior leaders in the NSW Police about a new way of working with the community. I remember at the end of one presentation a chief inspector who I liked and respected said, 'Thanks very much, Christine. What you just said means that everything I've ever done in my career has been a waste of time.' I replied, 'That's not true. I didn't imply that at all.' His comment back was, 'Maybe that's not what you said, but that was what I heard.'

You need to understand that you must be careful with what you say because it may be different from what people hear. That conversation also helped me realise that you don't have to tread on the past to get to a different future. Even if you don't intend to cause offence, it is important to respect the efforts people have already made to achieve valued outcomes.

Similarly, it is important to recognise where people come from. Attitudes and approaches reflect the period and place in which they grew up and were trained. Victoria Police in 2001 encompassed four generations across its 13,000 people. Though the average age was thirty-eight, there were people who'd spent forty years in policing alongside those who'd grown up in the 1980s and were just starting out. Aside from their careers in policing, they ran families, community groups, businesses and so on. Respecting these people with all their skills and experience was central to the way I wanted to engage them in reforming policing in Victoria.

In 2001, in the early days of my tenure as Commissioner, I requested that meetings be arranged with employees—uniformed and support—in different police stations and offices. I'm sure my first location, Frankston, was chosen so I would be deterred in my commitment to directly meet employees and hear their concerns. I explained who I was, talked about my family background in policing and stated some clear ground rules of the way we might proceed together. I said that I would and I hoped they would be respectful, without an 'us and them' attitude. We needed to work together and I was genuine in wanting to hear from them without deference to rank or privilege.

I then opened to questions and concerns, starting with a question: 'So if you'd got my job, what should we be working on to improve Victoria Police?' Off they went without much hesitation! Fifty issues were raised. After several months of doing the same thing—visiting police stations and workplaces all over Victoria, getting other senior managers out and using email to ask for people to nominate concerns—we managed to accumulate over five hundred issues that needed to be addressed. By the conclusion, I had met over six thousand members in their workplaces—in small one-person stations and in larger groups of three to four hundred people. At the end, my colleagues and I wondered how we would meet their expectations.

I'd been warned that members would only complain and whinge if I proceeded on this tack of asking them. We had indeed heard from a lot of people and now had a big list. But something else very important had been achieved. I'd taken the opportunity to show that I was concerned about and respected employees in all roles and parts of the organisation, that I was keen to listen and learn. I knew that some of the issues raised could be solved as 'quick wins', which would generate further confidence and goodwill that we would act on suggestions. For the more complex ones, I had some ideas on where the organisational intelligence might be to start working on and solving them. But there were also surprises—for example, a long-term female employee who had worked out a better system of transfers in and out of country stations just needed to be given the opportunity to share her thinking.

2 Understand an organisation's history and its people

To initiate change, I knew I needed to understand the history of Victoria Police—to use Amanda's phrase, 'to go forward you first need to go back'.[2] This required me to read media reports and publications and to ask lots of questions. Where had Victoria Police come from—why was it invented and how did systems and practices come to be in place? What did it do well? What were the unspoken rules and challenges? What were its successes and failures? Being a newcomer enables you to ask a lot of apparently innocent questions and listen closely to responses, including what is said, hinted at and not said.

I also needed to meet all the senior team. Interviewing the top sixty senior managers, I began to identify the trusted navigators and advisers to guide me. Senior management teams are a powerful group and can make or break a change program. We discussed in groups the challenges facing us, our organisation's history and what we did well and what we did poorly, the strengths and capacities we should build on, and what they would do if they had got my job. What people tell you individually and what they will volunteer in groups can be very different.

As a new leader and outsider, it was vital to learn about the history but not be bound or held hostage by traditional expectations and ways of doing things. The interviews helped me understand 'where the bodies were buried'—usually not literal bodies but the issues and secrets, loyalties and alliances that made sense of what had happened in the past. My discussions also guided me on which issues I needed to respect and which ones I needed to be open to investigating and finding out more about, or else they might continue to poison our culture and our efforts to change.

Even with a great deal of support from good people who didn't wish me to bump into or trip over the past, there were occasions when it became unavoidable. On the other hand, being an outsider meant I wasn't wedded to the past. I didn't have allegiances to groups or agendas. When I tackled sacred cows, I could feel many in the organisation sighing with relief and tacitly giving me their support.

We also determined that not just me, but other members of the senior team would go out into the workforce and spend time with staff in their offices. We went to police stations, participated in police patrols, and visited the specialists and professional support staff on their turf to listen. We set out to give everyone a chance to tell us what would make Victoria Police the best it could be.

Although part of our focus in all of this was internal, I was also seeking to nourish new relationships externally, with our stakeholders. My colleagues and I accepted many invitations from groups all over Victoria to speak at breakfasts, lunches and dinners. We met with members of local government, religious organisations, service organisations, educational and training providers, members of the business community and corporates who we thought we could learn from.

There was a further purpose being served through this process of listening and learning. Professor Mark Moore from the Kennedy School of Government suggests part of being a public sector leader is creating public value. To be empowered to deliver public value, an agency and its leaders need to be given legitimacy to do so from the authorising environment, including politicians, other agencies, stakeholders and community groups. It is this collection of groups who decide a leader and their organisation can be trusted and given the power and authority to bring about a change and tackle a problem or valued public goal.

By this stage in the change process I knew we had clear goals to reduce crime, make people safer, reduce the road toll and fix the problems identified by the members. Through the external and internal consultations, we were building legitimacy in the government and the community to tackle important issues. This external momentum and legitimacy can, in turn, build internal capability—a feeling that we could be courageous—and the capacity to achieve our goals.

3   Exploit timing and appetites for change

Victoria Police had been through some years of turmoil when I joined. They had lost a significant number of members due to budget cuts imposed by the then Liberal Government. A newly elected, young Labor Government had recently been voted in with a demonstrable enthusiasm for change. Even though Labor did not have a majority but governed with three independents, they were willing to sponsor change. Choosing an outsider sent a signal to the organisation and the community that things could change, that the government hoped someone with a different background, in this case a woman, one from New South Wales, would bring innovative ideas and fresh energy. It gave me a mandate that I consistently drew upon.

Victoria Police had always had a good relationship with the community but for some years had been subject to criticism from the media, the Police Association and others within the broader community. It became clear to me that I needed to talk to the community to understand their concerns and to develop positive relationships with the multiple stakeholders. I needed to help build trust and confidence that I was, indeed, going to introduce change and focus on neglected issues that communities and stakeholders cared about for example, domestic violence. Pressure from within and without gives you the best chance to bring about change. I needed external pressures of government, community groups and businesses as well as internal pressure from staff and members to mobilise change.

4   Send signals that reinforce the values you want to promote

Not long after it was announced that I'd had become the new Chief Commissioner of Victoria Police I received a telephone call from the Acting Commissioner. He said that the Justice Department had called him and were proposing that my swearing-in, which was to take place in a few weeks, be a big, public occasion. The department proposed that they would invite members of the community, members of parliament and a range of people from within Victoria Police. I would be sworn in by the Chief Magistrate and it would probably be televised. I asked him how other chief commissioners had been sworn in. He explained it was usually a small ceremony at the Leadership Centre with some members of the executive team and the appointee's family. I asked him what he recommended and he said the smaller occasion would be best, that I should follow the traditions that had been in place for many years.

When I tell this story, as I've done now several times to different audiences, I ask what they would have done: the public occasion or the smaller, traditional one. I recently presented the idea to a group of university students in a leadership program. I asked them to vote on which option they'd choose. Five voted for the big public occasion and thirty-five for the smaller traditional swearing-in ceremony. In another group, one involved in the automotive industry, eight suggested the big event and the other thirty the traditional model. In an executive development program group about fifteen voted for the public event and about thirty-five for the more traditional model.

I hadn't previously thought about using this story to illustrate how, even in some cases before you officially start, you are sending signals to an organisation and its stakeholders, including the community, about how you are going to proceed and what matters to you. When I ask participants why some chose the smaller, traditional occasion the reasons I generally get are:

- you don't want to a standout

- you want to fit into the way things are always done

- you want to show respect for the culture of the organisation and its customary processes

- as the first woman, you don't want to be seen behaving differently from the male incumbents

- you want to show you cannot be manipulated by the politicians or the marketers, that you want to be seen as your own person.

Those who chose the big, public occasion suggest that as a leader you want to signal that:

- change is likely

- you want to be more transparent

- you will represent the whole community and you're looking for their support.

I chose the big public occasion and I also chose to use that as an opportunity to give a very public speech about the kind of person I am. I said I was a citizen, a constable, a spouse, a daughter and a woman, and all those roles were very important to me and I would continue to value all that I was and my experiences in doing my job and making my decisions. It turned out to be a very impactful and highly remembered speech by many, especially in the community. It was covered widely by the media. On the other hand, I found out later that most police had no idea how the commissioner was sworn in and didn't seem to care anyway.

The lesson for me in this situation was to not be afraid of doing things differently because of what insiders might think. The swearing-in wasn't something that rank-and-file police put much value on, but the community certainly did.

5 Care

In the early stages of my time in Victoria Police I was asked by police members of the gay and lesbian community to march with them in the Pride March that was held in 2002. I accepted without hesitation, given that these members needed support, were doing a good job and had asked me. I didn't quite understand the implications of this decision until sometime afterwards. Once my decision became public, I received over eight hundred emails from members of the organisation, in the main expressing their anger and regret that I had decided to march. Various popular media commentators and outlets were enraged or baffled and there was a fair amount of scaremongering about what would follow if I marched. Although I came under pressure to change my decision, I kept reiterating that I had been asked and that one of my commitments was to support all policing members trying to do the right thing.

I did march with them and again received front-page publicity and much commentary on nightly news and talkback programs. The signal that was sent was simply that I would support members of Victoria Police no matter their gender, cultural background or sexuality, as long as they were doing a good job. To the community, it came to mean that I was my own person, that I was a strong supporter of diversity, and that I would stand up for people.

During my tenure, we also commenced plans for a significant number of police stations to be revamped or built. By the time, I'd left Victoria Police over two hundred police stations had been rebuilt or built, providing safer, more comfortable and more conducive conditions for employees. This $300 million program conducted over about ten years also had external impacts. The station-building program was designed to reflect a community orientation. Stations were not all the same but various architects were engaged to consult with and design buildings that were part of their communities. They became places the public felt pleased were there, confident to come into (if willingly!) and seek help from. Many were in country locations, which demonstrated the government's commitment to rural and regional communities.

The other key lesson, which is supported by a lot of research, is that seemingly small actions by leaders showing care for employees can have a huge impact. One example that we faced in Victoria Police included putting in extra resources and going the extra mile to support police and citizens who had been killed and injured in a bus crash in Egypt. A second was to bring home the body of one of our inspectors who had died climbing a mountain in Tibet.

6   Create a fertile environment for change

Good gardeners don't throw seeds on to hard ground and expect them to flourish. The same applies to those wanting to bring about long-term change. What are the organisational equivalents of preparing for change and growth? You create the environment by listening, drawing on the organisation's experiences and history, its failures and successes, and the willingness of many people to think about how the future could be better. You do things to empower people and give them confidence to initiate change. For example, when we set up task forces to work on the issues that had been identified by initial consultations, I requested that all task forces reflect the diverse range of people and skills in the organisation. These cross-functional, cross-geographical and multi-level teams produced champions—people with ability and enthusiasm—who could drive change and inspire others in all parts of our organisation.

I knew there were many in the organisation who believed we could be much better than we were. I encouraged people to email me directly with issues they cared about. Although there were a lot of emails, once I had demonstrated I was approachable, people told me many very useful and important things. I could then honour their trust by, to the best of my and the organisation's ability, doing something about what they shared with me.

7   Pay attention to the reasons for change

There are many reasons for organisations to change: new appointments, new or emerging issues, crises, budget cutbacks, new research, new challenges, change of direction or simply better ways that things could be done. People need a good reason to get involved in change. They might not like the reason but at least by having various people articulating the need for change, you can provide a foundation for them to understand what they might be facing and, importantly, why it is being done.

Research indicates that when we are trying to lead change, sometimes we focus too much on the overt, formal levers for change, such as structures and technical processes, while giving too little attention to the history and the informal norms and habits. If you think of an organisation as an iceberg, we pay most attention to the visible 10 per cent: the formal strategies, structures and systems. Yet success is more likely to depend on paying attention to the less visible 90 per cent. Here lies the real power, including beliefs about 'the way we do things around here', the shared stories, fears and unwritten control mechanisms. Also invisible, but similarly vital, is attending to language and signals, to take into account how those in the organisation read and hear what you're trying to do and what you say.

8 Look for leverage: 'Lifting the elephant'

While there were many pressing areas needing cultural change in Victoria Police, it was important that senior management and I did not get daunted by the scale of the task and what we were trying to do. Scepticism about the possibility of change was the default mindset for many with long tenures in the organisation. It wasn't enough for just me and a few of my colleagues to talk about the need for change. It was important to get individuals from around the organisation to think change was possible and act on it—to use a metaphor, to find ways to 'lift the elephant'. We couldn't get it up in one go but we could get several parts of it moving.

This approach informed how we proceeded. Of the 500 issues raised in our early consultations, we amalgamated them into eighty projects and then called for volunteers. Leaders for each project were chosen and people from all the different parts of the organisation with an interest were assigned to work on them and come back with a viable way forward within three months. They reported to a large senior meeting. Everyone took it seriously and came up with excellent, implementable recommendations.

Another opportunity arose when I learned that I would be required to report the previous year's crime statistics to the community and government. Crime rates had been climbing for some years and the figures looked appalling. I invited, in some cases nominated, colleagues to take responsibility for a particular issue of concern. In a couple of cases, when someone I knew would be capable but reluctant, I put it this way: 'Greatness has descended upon you!' I then encouraged them to define aspects of the issue they felt strongly about and set goals that we both agreed upon. They joined me at a press conference the following week when I announced to the media and community that these four senior officers would be taking responsibility on behalf of Victoria Police and the community reducing the crime or for working out how to improve our response. The categories chosen were stolen motor vehicles, breaking into premises, robberies and family violence.

9   Set goals and hold people accountable

Setting out some clear directions, breaking the work into manageable chunks and dealing with simple issues first can make the change process less daunting and more manageable. Research suggests that what people want when they go to work is:

- to know that someone (perhaps leadership) knows where the organisation is going

- to understand how their job or role contributes to a worthwhile whole

- good management that will help them get the job done.

Having people clearly understand goals and accountabilities requires a lot of ongoing communication. Today technology can assist in this process but nothing beats sharing the data personally, with presentations and a preparedness to be open and transparent.

Whatever the goals are, I find that if they are clearly articulated, such as in our case reducing crime and serious injury on the road, people in the organisation respond. Visibly holding people accountable for delivering against those goals is also important. Telling people what needs to be done, but not how, empowers members to try new ways of working.

The eighty task forces that were set up after our consultations were assigned with reporting back ways to solve or mitigate particular issues. Sometimes when I am working with audiences, I ask them to estimate what proportion of task forces reported back. Often people think only a small proportion did. But each one in Victoria Police did, and this provides an important insight. If you give a task and demonstrate trust that senior management will listen, people in all parts of the organisation will step up. The clear majority in the police had excellent suggestions and wanted to contribute.

Some of their recommendations were adopted straight away, others became part of a five-year strategic plan. Of the four key crime areas that were identified, we saw significant reductions in three: robberies, stolen motor vehicles and break-and-enters. In the fourth, the more intractable area of reducing family violence, we developed a better co-ordinated response that was implemented across Victoria and involved several government departments.

We also introduced a process called Compstat, a model of accountability that had previously been used in New York City and other parts of the United States. Various statistical indicators were adopted to compare the performance of different divisions or departments against previous performance and against each other. Instituting these systems and similar scorecards helped focus our efforts and also delivered clear messages about our progress to external stakeholders, especially government. These measures thus enhanced our authorising environment, the confidence of government and our licence to keep going and tackle new things.

10 Research: consult it, do it and share it

It might seem obvious that good policies and practices should be underpinned by research, but that's not always the case. Victoria Police was confronted by a range of challenges, from counterterrorism to family violence, sexual assault and organised crime, but had not accessed or commissioned research about these issues on behalf of the community. Across a range of issues, we began to form partnerships with academics and universities, corporates and other agencies to undertake research. We commissioned consultants to help us think through resource allocation models to better target and use our resources. The establishment of a counterterrorism unit at Monash University included early studies on deradicalisation. This centre went on to provide continuing counterterrorism research for Australia on how to deploy resources and combat emerging forms of radicalisation such as social media channels.

I have always been a great supporter of the reform of systems. We often take good people and give them poor systems to operate within. Much of an employee's effectiveness is determined by the systems they work in. In my experience, and research backs this up, at least 80 per cent of the problems come from 20 per cent of the systems and locations. If you can find remedies for these systems issues, it delivers a big boost to effectiveness and productivity.

As part of a continuous improvement focus we commissioned a significant amount of research on topics ranging from family violence to organised crime, sexual assault, traffic management, juvenile justice, organisational reform, financial management and several other areas. The results of this research and our participation in it meant we were up to date with best practice in policing around the world. At one point, we had over twenty different research grants with universities throughout Australia and in some parts of the United States. We tried to ensure that our policy formulation was underpinned by the research and the experience of the members involved and the community. For instance, in working on counterterrorism we formed a multi-faith advisory committee and a broader community advisory group, and accessed academics involved in writing about terrorism issues to help us formulate the best way forward. When we became aware of some major psychological issues facing members, we trained over six hundred civilians and police officers as peer support counsellors. The evidence that this was the way forward came from psychological research and experience in other police organisations.

Another example of creating system-wide momentum for change was the creation of the Australia New Zealand Policing Advisory Agency (ANZPAA) to share best practice in policing across the region. It's good policy to learn what others have already done, but historically there had been fiefdoms within sections of the police and resistance to learning from other jurisdictions.

11 Develop good management

Managers can make an enormous difference in people's lives, and bad managers can stuff up people—I've certainly seen my share of the latter. Many business and government organisations spend an enormous amount of time and money on teaching people how to manage. It's not that complicated. Simply put, it's how you'd like to be treated yourself.

In Victoria Police, we developed a range of programs designed to improve managers' skills and leadership capacities, we moved people to various positions to expand their skills and, on some occasions, took people out of management positions when they were better suited for other, perhaps more technical roles. We also provided mentors, including volunteers from corporate organisations, so that managers might be assisted in developing their capacities to reflect on their own behaviours and how they might be impacting on those they managed.

Other ways we improved management skills included encouraging all our employees to seek further education and training, to join management and leadership programs where they would sit alongside, learn from and develop networks with effective managers in the private and not-for-profit sectors. Policing had often been treated as a 'for life' career, where formal education was less relevant than on-the-job experience. We set about changing those norms by encouraging training and education of all kinds, as well as fostering links with providers.

12 Keep perspective

Change is hard and challenges most of us. The leader who is an agent of change has enemies in those who have done well under the previous regime, and 'lukewarm defenders' in those who may do well under the new order. Remember that if you are involved in leading something new or different you will always face opposition.

Both organisations and individuals often restrict themselves in what they might achieve. The limits can come from previous experiences as well as personal and organisational history, or fear of failure or ridicule. Challenging organisations and people to overcome their limits and barriers requires leaders to accept that there are personal risks and that there will be losses—of power, expertise, face, confidence.

Leading change requires recognition of these limits and a belief in people to overcome barriers. At crucial times, it also helps to step back, gain perspective and have around you people you care about and who care about you. For me that was and is my father, partner John, friends and colleagues who remind me of the important things—that life will go on. My mother used to tell me that, if things turned out badly, 'You can always come home'. I'd say to myself, 'I can always drive a bus.'

It's been suggested that I would have had a much easier time in policing if I had just left things alone, if I'd just gone with the flow. But that was not my way, nor would it have been good leadership to be frightened to take on the problems or the opportunities for change I saw. These twelve lessons helped me lead that change.

5
Leadership in difficult times

In Whittlesea, one day soon after the fire emergency had passed, I came across an old woman wandering near the crowded chaos at the emergency relief centre. She looked shocked and bedraggled and her feet were bare and filthy with ash. 'We'll get you some shoes,' I told her in my most reassuring tones, dropping a comforting hand on her shoulder. 'Why?' she said, looking at me quizzically. I haven't worn shoes for twenty years.' Here was my lesson. Never assume you know what people want, or need.

Christine Nixon, 2011

Many types of difficulties beset organisations and require leadership. When we ask workshop participants for examples of difficult or tough times they've experienced, they volunteer a wide range, including major emergency situations such as environmental crises, volcano eruptions, floods and fire, tsunamis and cyclones. Those working in various parts of the world have also cited widespread disease, civil wars and uprisings, financial crises, corruption and treachery. In Australia, most examples of difficult times fit into three categories.

First are drastic organisational changes, such as restructuring, implementing and responding to cutbacks of resources, redundancies, the closure of agencies, and all the consequences of policy and political cycles that can make leadership hard. Next come events such as the death of employees, either at work or outside it, which can leave colleagues traumatised and shell shocked. The third category contains those disasters and crises that are unpredictable and require rapid emergency responses as well as management and leadership over the medium and longer term.

Leadership is critical in all these circumstances, though what is required may be different in each one. We draw on research and experiences to help identify the key tasks of leadership in varied examples. We also show that difficult times are often opportunities for change. Crises or setbacks show up the problems with the status quo. They demonstrate unequivocally the reasons why people can't just keep doing what they have always done. They can create a 'burning platform'—a reason or pretext for implementing much-needed change that can't be ignored—yet lack of courage, trust, agility or willingness to seize these chances means such change opportunities are often lost.

Defining difficult times

Research shows that, except for major physical, financial and other emergencies, crises are at least partially in the eye of the beholder—the affected employees, communities, clients and investors. What one individual identifies as a crisis, another may just see as business as usual. Two examples show this. For many years in Australia and elsewhere, family violence was not seen as a crisis. It took concerted action and leadership by many stakeholders—women's groups and refuge centres, individuals who are victims or affected, police and the law, housing, public health and social work—to mobilise the community and politicians to see family violence as a crisis deserving strong cross-sectoral action. In a second example of differing viewpoints, when Christine held discussions with people from the Solomon Islands about the impact cyclones and tsunamis had had on them, they said to her, 'That wasn't a crisis—that was part of everyday life.'

In many cases, crises or emergencies are given that status by the perceptions and responses of participants and other stakeholders. Those involved, including leaders, always have a stake in playing issues up or down. Although 'the facts' are important, it is how they are perceived—often against a backdrop of other circumstances—that will determine the appetite for remedial action and demanded responses. This is what makes leadership important.

Leaders can often play a key and productive role in shaping an organisational or community understanding and preparedness to change and respond to difficulty. Unless you explain quickly, accurately and with credibility what is occurring, the view of the event may be distorted dramatically by the media or by stakeholders with a particular interest. What often defines a crisis initially for participants—indeed, whether there even is a crisis—is the way in which one leader or a group of leaders handles the crisis and communicates a message about its implications and significance. An example from Christine's experience was that of police administrations usually playing down corruption issues with a 'nothing to see here' response. When notified of the drug squad corruption allegations in Victoria Police, she instead went public and announced a team to investigate, and another to consider the systems failures that led to the concerns. Being proactive in this way means you are being transparent and looking for support from outside to pressure change within. Similarly, the medium- and long-term response of leaders is often crucial to whether difficult times break careers, governments and organisations—or demonstrate their adaptability and resilience.

When operating in difficult times or crises, it is important to recognise that:

- facts and evidence are important but they don't always define a response

- a crisis can come from anywhere—what might be normal in one place would be a crisis in another

- a crisis is what people make of it, and actors have a stake in playing it up or down

- likely media and opposition responses will be to attack authorities and say, 'It was preventable', that 'There are no acts of God', 'Why didn't the plans work?' or 'Who's to blame?'

- a crisis never speaks for itself, and therefore an important role for leaders is to shape the understanding of affected groups and communities across time and through different stages

- communication and co-ordination are key for all involved

- you need to develop trust, empower others and accept help.

To expand on how you can lead in difficult times, we draw on six examples, starting with events involving a small number of people and concluding with the system-wide disaster of the 2009 Victorian bushfires.

1 A death or severe setback of an individual

Amanda and her colleague Fiona Haines, who is an academic criminologist, conducted research in the 1990s that looked at deaths in workplaces. The focus of this research was less on how the deaths happened and more on how organisations responded after they happened.[1] Most commonly, managers in those workplaces did not want to talk about the incident in order to 'move past it' or 'put it behind us'. Legal liability and insurance issues often reinforced this response of pulling down the shutters and saying as little as possible. On a psychological level this response is understandable—it is a way of dealing with shock and trauma. But it creates fear, anxiety or sadness among other employees that goes underground and often causes consequences later, and a barrier to prevent any organisational learning and change.

Our view is that when an organisation experiences an unexpected death, those in leadership need to pause, recognise it has occurred, and understand that it will have profound consequences. Colleagues and others who knew the deceased need to talk about what happened, they need information and time to mourn. The wider organisation will also be affected. Leaders will set the tone and be judged on how they handle the situation. When Christine heard about two employees of Victoria Police who were killed while in Egypt, she sent a team to support the families and others who had been injured. Even though the employees weren't engaged in Victoria Police business at the time, and weren't widely known, she knew it was the right thing to do.

Coping with death is always very hard and most leaders feel unqualified and inadequate to respond. Every situation is different, requiring a mix of support, resources and sensitivity to context. There is no one right approach. While external pressures may be to get over it and move on quickly, the opposite approach is how you provide leadership. Some very simple steps to do this include:

- recognising the significance of the event and, if possible, personally talking to those affected

- allowing people time to process the event

- seeking advice, support and resources from experts

- providing support of various kinds to those directly and indirectly affected.

These actions demonstrate that the leader cares and will use their influence, resources and capacity to support families. Leadership is judged on such actions.

2 Restructuring, cutbacks and redundancies

Employees can experience organisational reforms involving cutbacks and redundancies as traumatic. This is the case for both those who leave and those who remain. How tough this can be depends on the process, communications and options provided, such as whether voluntary redundancies are on the table. But even if leaders don't have much room to move, taking time and communicating reasons, consequences and timing of the changes is crucial.

In a recent and significant government downsizing involving massive redundancies, one department secretary stood out for the way she handled that process with her staff. The keys to her approach were to:

- treat people as adults able to handle the news, respond to it, and take up other options to redirect careers and lives

- keep people informed of the good and the bad news

- promise and deliver support, for example assistance to get alternative jobs, provide references and contacts

- allow the time needed and recognise that people will grieve

- recognise 'survivor guilt' and its consequences, that the people who retain their jobs also need support to feel confident and enthusiastic about the tasks ahead.

In addition to these lessons for leading groups through difficult downsizing or restructuring, it is also important to recognise that such events may provide invaluable opportunities to:

- reassess where the organisation is putting its energies and resources

- rearrange priorities

- put pressure on decision-makers about needed innovations or technological adaptations

- think about activities an area might stop doing, including those you've had doubts about prior to the changes.

3 A serious organisational failure

Early in her time as Chief Commissioner of Victoria Police, Christine was given a copy of the crime statistics as part of a general collection of information about the organisation. Conventional wisdom about Victoria Police was that it was a good, effective force without the corruption or serious problems that were coming to light in other police jurisdictions. Christine was always sceptical of such conventional wisdoms and the complacency that often surrounds them.

When she looked at the statistics, she was shocked that crime rates were on the rise and had been for many years. She was advised that shortly she would have to release the crime statistics to the community as part of the annual reporting cycle. One particular statistic and issue caught her eye. In 2001, 48,000 cars had been reported stolen in Victoria. The rate had been growing for many years and looked like heading up to 50,000 cars stolen the coming year. It was a shocking crime rate, yet many around her seemed to be thinking that they couldn't do much about it—after all, it was just stolen vehicles; they had other more serious crimes to deal with.

The requirement to report publicly gave Christine an opportunity to use that occasion to talk up the statistics rather than down, as her predecessors had done. It was an opportunity to commit publicly as well as send a clear message to the organisation that they were going to reform the way that stolen motor vehicles were tackled, alongside a range of other serious crime types that were also on the rise, such as robberies, break-and-enters, cases of malicious damage, and so on.

Christine chose a well-respected and capable member of the senior team to lead the response to stolen motor vehicles. Using one of her favoured terms, she advised that 'greatness was about to descend on him', and that she wanted him to lead a team to bring about a reduction in stolen vehicles. His first response was to suggest that it was impossible. They had tried lots of different techniques but nothing seemed to work. When she asked him to estimate his goal for reducing stolen motor vehicles, he volunteered 2 to 3 per cent. Christine suggested 20 per cent over the following year and went on to say that he was coming to a press conference with her in a few days to announce that he would be the new champion focusing on reducing the number of stolen vehicles.

Through this process, Christine also began to invite this person to think differently and more confidently about what processes and resources he might use to meet their new target. She had already thought about the problem and knew the typical circumstances of car theft. An important part of the exercise was helping this leader and his team and colleagues to recognise that there were many people in the community, in the motor vehicle industry, in the insurance industry and in the car-park industry—lots of cars were stolen from car parks—who would have intelligence to offer and would help police reduce this crime if they were invited in and consulted. The most surprising example of people's willingness to help happened when police invited a group of young but experienced car thieves in to talk to them, and they promptly told the police exactly where and how they stole vehicles and what they did next!

The result was a dramatic drop in the number of stolen motor vehicles. This approach became a template for many other categories of crime, from break-and-enters to family violence:

- Ensure the organisation knows and understands the statistics and cares about them, rather than feels ignorant, complacent or hopeless.

- Know that evidence is vital and organisations can hide behind inaccurate or incomplete data. At one point Christine announced a review of the crime statistics by an external agency. This helped her use data and evidence that was demonstrably seen as independent to mobilise people's attention and action.

- Encourage partnering to help those leading change initiatives to feel supported and to access wider resources, allies and partners—other agencies, cross-sector and industry support, community support, and even on occasion media support— to tackle big and difficult issues.

- Exert pressure for change, from within and without, on issues where urgent change is needed and growing concern about an organisation within the community and the media needs to be diffused. For example, announce initiatives to the media and share them with journalists rather than 'drip-feeding' them information.

- Choose the right person to lead the response. Christine nominated very different individuals as champions to lead different areas of crime response and ensured they were given support to step up to their higher media profile and be skilled in managing complex communications.

4 Responding to the crisis of family violence

Christine has had a career-long commitment to tackling family violence from her very early days in the NSW Police, when she became aware of violence against some female colleagues within the ranks and from extensive research while she was studying. Later, during various roles at Darlinghurst as a researcher and then as Region Commander, she came face-to-face with how endemic family violence was. This has given her a determination to make sure police do better in reducing the incidence of it. However, when she arrived at Victoria Police determined to have an impact on family violence, few outside of women's refuges and social work agencies saw it as a crisis.

In Victoria, significant underreporting of family violence made it hard to get police and political attention. Victims didn't report violence because often they received treatment from the police and judicial systems that was degrading and reinforced in them a sense of powerlessness. In the first instance, an *increase* in the incidence of reported family violence needed to be seen as a measure of progress by police. The issue at that time was also not a focus for government. The degree of difficulty was high and included bringing together agencies with very different cultures, histories of mistrust and institutional barriers, such as not sharing critical information about perpetrators and risks. People had been trying to break down these barriers for years, but working on family violence inevitably taps into the prejudices, histories and personal baggage of many, much of which is buried and not discussed.

Family violence can become normalised across whole communities where there has been a collective acceptance, silence or shame, and workers at many levels experience trauma and vicarious trauma. So how do you begin to mobilise effort on this crisis? Because it is emotional and brings so much up for people, leaders require particular skills; they need structures and their own support systems.

Research is building a bigger picture of the problem and solutions, especially following the federal and Victorian Royal commissions into institutional child sex abuse and family violence. Lessons from Christine's experience include:

- Take a system-wide view and look for leaders with formal roles and influence across sectors to recognise that the whole system needs reform. Plan ways to hold focus and accountabilities over time. Struggling to get government's attention to the issue, Christine decided to contact women politicians on both sides of politics and female heads and secretaries of departments, bringing them together to discuss how to move forward. The resulting group proved pivotal in ensuring the departments of justice, corrections and social services and other bodies were acting in concert.

- Gather data, evidence and research about what has worked overseas, about the health and other effects on women, and wider consequences on society and public expenditure. Ensure that the details are known widely through information, communications and the media.

- Make sure organisations working in the area, such as police, understand the costs. Approached by a victim of long-term family violence who wanted her to know what it was like, Christine decided to ask this woman if she would be prepared to be filmed, so that police officers could take in the fear and extreme difficulties for victims coming forward.

This was an important part of a much wider effort to train and support police to feel more confident in family violence situations, to give them practical protocols and guidance on how to follow through.

- Choose a well-respected champion to lead the efforts. In 2002, Commander Leigh Gassner was invited to Christine's office and asked to take on the role of leading a task force to develop the police, government and community response to family violence. A set of major reforms followed, which gained momentum from the wider community and the appointment of 2015 Australian of the Year Rosie Batty, who has been campaigning against family violence since her son was killed by his father.

5 Tackling dishonesty

Another category of leading in difficult times is identifying and taking steps against dishonest dealings or corruption within an organisation. When Christine became Chief Commissioner, there was a view that Victoria Police was less corrupt than some other forces in Australia. It took some time for Christine to discover where pockets of corruption lay in the organisation, especially as for many years the Victoria Police Armed Offenders Squad had been in the headlines for their 'crime-busting' work. Sometimes it was for their great work and major arrests, but at other times there were allegations of corruption and brutality. The squad regarded themselves as invincible and indispensable, able to operate according to different rules in their separate St Kilda Road headquarters.

As she has described in her memoir *Fair Cop*, Christine tried several measures to break the corrosive culture, including moving people in and out of the squad, before making the decision that the squad needed to be shut down. She was gravely concerned—and there was evidence—that they might kill someone. In 2006, a report by the Office of Police Integrity raising concerns about police violence was about to be released. This provided Christine with her opportunity and she acted quickly. Notifying the squad that she was coming with another senior officer, she asked that the senior members be gathered together. On her way to the meeting room, she felt the weight and power of this group—all around the corridor walls were media articles of the arrests they had made, the squad's long history and its heroes. Christine describes it as 'going into the belly of the beast'. But she needed to be prepared to front up physically and deliver a clear message, and this required her not to be intimidated. Her message to them was brief: she was shutting down the squad that day. They protested about who would make the big arrests, and she responded by saying there were many other officers who could do that.

The following day, she received a phone call from a radio commentator, who was live to air and said he had a recording that would end her career. She asked what it was and was told that someone had taped her meeting with the Armed Offenders Squad. The radio host knew he could not legally play it on air without her permission. Christine knew what she had said and so felt no qualms about allowing it to be aired. After playing the recording the rather sheepish presenter thanked her and she wished him and his listeners good morning.

As it turned out, allowing the recording to be played on live radio was a bonus. It showed a well-respected leader taking a stand that was consistent with the overarching values and mission of the police. It wasn't a vendetta, however much some individuals sought to present it as one. It sent a powerful message to the rest of the organisation, the community and stakeholders, including government, that corruption and violence would not be tolerated no matter how powerful or influential those involved were.

6   Bushfire recovery and reconstruction

In February 2009, Victoria faced a disaster. Extreme weather conditions in the months before February, a prolonged drought and extremely low rainfall became the setting for a catastrophic series of bushfires. Fires had been burning in Victoria through January, but 7 February saw an outbreak of over a thousand fires as temperatures soared 12 to 18 degrees above the average. The city of Melbourne recorded 46.4°C, its highest temperature on record. With a combination of strong and gusty winds, low humidity and high record temperatures, the stage was set for extreme fire conditions. Six main fire complexes spread across the state. Then a severe cool change exacerbated the situation. Fire spotting was up to 25 kilometres in front of the main fire front, when typically they would be just 2 kilometres out in front. The fires continued to burn until early March.

Kevin Tolhurst, an academic from Melbourne University, said the conditions were the worst you could experience. The fires created energy equivalent to 1500 atomic bombs of the size dropped on Hiroshima. The impact, determined months afterwards, included 173 fatalities, a smaller but considerable number of burned and injured people, 2133 properties destroyed, 1500 properties damaged and 106 communities in 25 municipalities affected, in some cases completely destroyed. Over 430,000 hectares of land was burned, over 8000 stock lost and at least 12,500 kilometres of fencing damaged. The wildlife loss was estimated at over one million animals.

Very quickly after the fires the Victorian Government created the Victorian Bushfire Appeal Fund, which in a relatively short period raised over $388 million. It also announced a Royal Commission to inquire into the cause of and response to the fires, and the establishment with the federal government of the Victorian Bushfire Reconstruction and Recovery Authority (VBRRA). The Victorian premier then asked Christine to chair the Authority as she had such strong support in the community, who trusted she would lead the recovery with care and effectiveness. VBRRA became responsible for co-ordinating the largest rebuilding and recovery program in the state's history and focused on four key areas: people's wellbeing, reconstruction, local economies and the environment. All these aspects had at their heart the communities affected.

Responding to the disaster required multiple approaches, focusing on both immediate needs and long-term response. Initially, emergency relief was given priority before recovery and reconstruction. The recovery and reconstruction framework adopted came from a range of emergency response and recovery experiences from New Zealand and Victoria (see Figure 5.1).

Figure 5.1: Reconstruction and recovery framework

The Victorian Bushfire Reconstruction and Recovery Authority is using a recognised disaster recovery framework and has designed some overall guiding principles to govern activities.

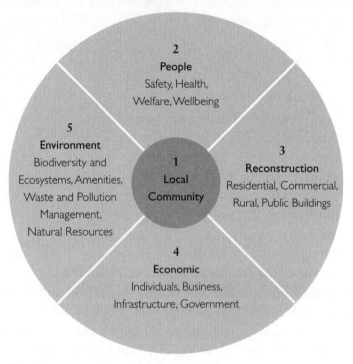

Guiding Principles

As a starting point for the framework the following guiding principles will govern the overall activities of the Authority through the recovery process:

Welfare
The safety and welfare of people in the local community including householders, volunteers and workers will be the top-level priority and will not be compromised.

Meeting Needs
Resources for recovery will be focused on areas of greatest need in each community.

Community Engagement
Community involvement is key and will be pursued through all activities, with management at the local level empowered to deliver results.

Integrity
Provision of services and resources will be governed by the principles of fairness and equity.

Tailored Solutions
The needs of each community impacted by the fires are different and the recovery solutions will be tailored to the specific needs of each community.

Christine learned from the bushfire recovery how important leadership in emergency situations is, and her key lessons include:

- nominating who's in charge and who will be the spokespersons for the disaster

- providing food, water, housing and safety as priorities

- providing information and establishing community engagement as soon as possible—calling community meetings to both give and receive information

- looking for any ready-made plans that local government or state emergency services might have in place to adopt or adapt, but remaining agile and responsive to circumstances

- ensuring co-ordination of all levels of government by getting senior people together quickly; for example, in the case of New Zealand earthquakes where heads of agencies head to the 'beehive', a central office close to parliament

- establishing levels of power, authority and budget

- having mechanisms to co-ordinate volunteers and donations, and encourage those who wish to help to register and to donate funds to an appeal rather that giving clothes or household goods that are harder to process and distribute

- establishing community service hubs where services such as volunteer, insurance and government advice can be accessed in one place by those affected

- collecting data as soon as possible for briefings to government and media on a daily then weekly or monthly basis as is appropriate

- keeping records of progress—VBRRA reported to government monthly for five years after the fires—as for many years after devastating emergencies it remains important to know where money has gone and whether there are residual funds from government and non-government sources that need to be spent.

Academic and author Professor Paul 't Hart and his coauthors, focus their research on leadership in times of crisis, and stress that these are always opportunities for leaders.[2] They suggest all crises have stages such as the following nine, and each requires different responses:

1. What's happening, and what might happen next? Simple explanations of the situation are needed. Identify what things might happen next; for example, what we know and don't know, when will the crisis subside, what's the size of the problem, who's affected, when someone will be appointed to take charge and when food, shelter and support will be available.

2. What are we doing now and how we will get through this? Responses can emphasise: we have people on the ground, we are assessing the situation, this kind of help is coming, we are setting up recovery centres, and we will get through this.

3. What choices do we have to make? A response might set out the options, or state that there is only one way to deal with the situation. Restrictions and warnings may be required, such as don't drink the water, don't go to certain places.

4. Shape the direction—leaders can begin providing a narrative about what's happening, such as 'this crisis is manageable', 'we know what we are dealing with', 'this provides us with opportunities to do/build better next time'.

5. What we have done—communicate actions and provide information in different forms, such as describing what help has been brought in and how many relief locations have been set up.

6. What are the outcomes we are trying to achieve? Identify feasible outcomes over a particular period and encourage people to be realistic about which businesses and communities can be re-established in what time periods.

7. Bring the crisis to closure by re-establishing new routines and a sense of the 'new normal'.

8. State that you are on track to fix outstanding problems and issues.

9. Review lessons learned and opportunities for reform.

After the Victorian bushfires, there was extensive research on many aspects of the crisis but one area that we wish to draw attention to looked at the responses through a gender lens. As discussed at the end of the preceding chapter, one of the things that this research found was that men were more likely to stay and defend their properties (often with tragic consequences) while women were more likely to follow official advice and leave. The researchers argued that, especially for some men, 'leadership' in this high-danger situation equated literally standing firm and being heroic, while leaving was seen as weakness. Because of this, it has been recommended that training, especially for men, is needed to help people understand that leadership in a crisis can include behaviours that are not typically seen as 'heroic', such as consulting and seeking information, asking for help and caring.

Similarly, international research from a gender point of view notes how narratives of and learning about successful crisis management often emphasise the contribution of individual heroes and higher-level management, while collective achievements and the roles, often played by women, of caring and providing basic comfort and services are often undervalued. Indeed, research suggests that crisis management suffers from the historic dominance of militaristic, masculine models of leadership that are often unsuitable for the particularities and context of disasters. This is another example of the issue we described earlier, in that we need to pay close attention to how the story of leadership is told. In crisis management, the story of leadership may effectively be limited or distorted by a focus on individual heroes, downplaying the collective, practical and caring activities that are essential to communities re-establishing.

As someone who observed Christine's leadership through difficult times at Victoria Police and after the bushfires, Amanda noticed that Christine practised a particular form of leadership that involved a lot of 'on the ground' listening to and talking with those affected, not just the officials or the self-designated leaders. Quite frequently, people were very emotional and likely to lash out, so these situations demanded courage and a conviction that she needed to be there, to pay attention and commit to respond. There is no substitute for this personal embodied presence (see also chapter 10). In the aftermath of the bushfires Christine, her partner John, and her assistants, spent weeks and then months on the ground in bushfire-affected communities. They traversed huge areas, came to know the locals well and have stayed in touch with many of the people affected. Hopefully, this enhanced the community's confidence that support would be forthcoming, that communities would be rebuilt, that they wouldn't be forgotten.

Many of these situations involved a lot of straight talk, too. Some things may never recover. People needed to make hard decisions about whether to pick up families, businesses and lives and move elsewhere. Practicality was needed, not sentimentality. Christine communicated a confidence that people could and would make the necessary changes. Another part of her role was co-ordinating the efforts—in some cases 'appearances'—of politicians, volunteers and high-profile people whose value in visiting was not always clear. Again, this required a steely focus on what mattered, dispensing with egos and extracting the maximum practical assistance for the victims from all the assorted offers.

These experiences—as well as research[3]—show that we should never underestimate the importance in leadership of a preparedness to care, to listen and to be physically present, in empowering others in difficult times.

6
Influencing and enabling

Lifting as you climb ...

Joan Kirner and Moira Rayner, 1999

A key aspect of leadership is the capacity to influence others—bosses, friends, colleagues, clients, communities and opponents—towards potentially beneficial outcomes. Leaders also need to build behind-the-scenes support for ideas to ensure initial buy-in and ongoing ownership of initiatives. While influencing is pivotal, we also want to focus on enabling; that is, encouraging and giving confidence to others to try new things, whether they are more junior, a peer or superior, or an external stakeholder or ally.

Christine developed an interest in research on influencing because much of her success has been based on the power to persuade in situations where she knew that she couldn't rely on her position or sanctions to foster openness to innovation. She has often also felt frustrated that great ideas and reforms fail because people don't know how to use subtle processes of encouragement and persuasion.

We draw on research and experience to explore how to influence and enable, beginning with psychological approaches—those that encourage us to understand what makes people tick, and to customise our efforts in influencing to people's styles and preferences. Then, we explore more politically oriented approaches, those that focus on how to gain power, especially in situations where formal authority may be opposed to change. The third section in this chapter distils approaches that have been effective in Christine's and Amanda's experiences from the perspective of women leading.

Psychological research and approaches

Hugh Mackay is a social researcher who has written extensively on the behaviour of Australians and our communities. In the book *What Makes Us Tick*, his research identifies ten desires or needs he believes we all have and are important in understanding how we can influence others.[1] They include the need to belong, to connect and to be useful. Christine finds that drawing on these desires is a helpful reminder of the commonality among people, that we all share some relatively simple needs, and recognising these needs can guide the implementation of organisational change. Conversely, if we see people as unwilling to change, as resistant or perhaps not up to the task, then no change is probably what will happen. If we've already made the judgements, dismissed those people and their capacity to change, then that's what we'll likely get back from them. People's resistance can come from their history, fear, not wanting to stand out and cynicism learned from bitter experience. It is always valuable to understand that and help them to see opportunities differently.

A second body of psychological research on influencing others encourages us to tailor how and what we ask of them to the type of person they are. In her meetings with police officers at all levels, Christine found it helpful to consider in advance, for example, their age, experience and interests, and tailor her conversations accordingly. Is an individual determined and strong-willed or quiet and analytical? Do they prefer to read the material first or do they prefer an animated presentation? Do they like small talk or just the facts? On Monday mornings, would they like you to talk about what happened on the weekend for their football team or just make sure you get to the point, taking less time than is allocated?

These are important things to think about when you try to influence someone's behaviour. When she headed Victoria Police, Christine worked with Boston Consulting Group (BCG) on strategies to combat organised crime; their presentations to her on a regular basis were short, sharp and clear and set out the progress they were making against the goals that had been set. These seemed to hit a sweet spot with her. BCG, who might normally present an extensive PowerPoint deck of information and analytical slides, increasingly tailored their presentations and report to suit the mix of issues that Christine was interested in and their mutually evolving understanding of how to tackle those issues. Through recent feedback from one of the BCG partners, it turned out that they too enjoyed these sessions because they understood that she was absolutely committed to improving the way Victoria Police dealt with organised crime.

Psychological research shows individuals can be broadly categorised into particular style types, and there are many widely used schemata that have demonstrated the validity of these categories if they are used judiciously and respectfully. Christine has drawn on the research of psychologist David Merrill to understand herself and others better. His style categories of 'expressive', 'amiable', 'driver' and 'analytical' suggest different influencing strategies that will appeal, from telling stories and entertaining through to providing logical, well-researched proposals.[2] This research is a reminder of the need to tailor your approach to the other person's preference rather than defaulting to your own. Over time certain role styles and their mix might change. While Christine was Police Commissioner the analytical and driver traits dominated. Now that she works for herself with less political and media scrutiny, her expressive side has become more dominant.

Another body of work that Christine has found helpful comes from author Robert Cialdini, who sets out six simple ideas to consider when influencing: liking, reciprocity, consensus, consistency, authority and scarcity.[3] As an example, for consensus he suggests finding common experiences when influencing. It is useful to invoke authority of different kinds—expertise, research, past experience—and this can be especially important for women, who are held to a higher hurdle of authoritativeness. These approaches always need to be employed respectfully, with the emphasis on listening and understanding rather than treating individuals or groups as means to your ends. People have good barometers for manipulative tactics and will withdraw openness if they suspect they are being played or used—which brings us to another body of politically based research on influencing.

Political approaches

Books have been written for centuries about how to win power, how to bring groups around, how to handle enemies and deal with opposition. The writings of Renaissance historian and philosopher Niccoló Machiavelli in *The Prince*[4] and fifth-century BC Chinese warrior Sun Tzu in *The Art of War* are often cited in business and leadership. There is wisdom in these writings even though we may disagree with how power was exercised. For example, in Chinese and other Asian martial arts the dictum is that while you must keep supporters close, you must keep enemies closer, stressing the importance of knowing the capabilities and motivation of the opposition. Consistent with the message of our previous chapter, Sun Tzu argued that 'in the midst of chaos there is opportunity'.

During her studies, Christine was introduced to an American writer of the 1960s and 1970s, Saul Alinsky.[5] His work guided some radical and community activism that occurred in the United States, United Kingdom and Australia through those decades. Alinsky followed a tradition of helping the poor and disadvantaged to organise themselves to tackle issues, such as halting the demolition of old communities for redevelopment, creating better health and education services, fighting racism and resisting wars and conscription. He identified thirteen 'Rules for Radicals' that were designed to help people who were often placed in extreme situations to fight oppressive authorities.[6] There is wisdom in the rules about running campaigns for change—for example, using tactics that your people enjoy (rule 6) and keeping the pressure on (rules 7 and 8). For Christine, there are three rules that are particularly relevant to leadership: numbers 1, 4 and 5.

Rule 1: Power is not what you have, but what the enemy (or opposition) thinks you have

This is very helpful when you're feeling disempowered or not sure of the way to go forward. If you think you're strong enough, able enough and can self-authorise yourself to do something, do it! The people you are trying to convince might wonder who authorised you to do whatever you are doing, but you are self-authorising, and that is something all leaders must do from time to time. The power comes from within you.

When Christine talks to people about this issue she often suggests that some of the most powerful people she knows are not those running organisations. The CEO or the leadership team is sometimes the least empowered and the most likely to place limits on themselves about what is possible. Some of the most powerful people she's seen are those in the mid levels of organisations—those who have nothing to lose as they see it, and who just get on and do what they believe is necessary and ethical regardless of the consequences. She often tells the story of a young senior constable from a very tough background who decided she wanted to do something about young people who commit crimes. She wanted to have more of them diverted from the criminal justice system to be allowed another chance. Her purpose and drive, informed by her personal experience and knowledge, helped her overcome many hurdles that were put in her way.

This rule also applies to the enemy's view of your resources. When Christine was part of an organisation for many years that had a small group of members, they behaved like they had hundreds of members, publishing a newsletter, running conferences and giving awards. They had connections with international networks and invited international guests to visit. They garnered much more influence than they should have been entitled to due to their size, and became known as 'the mouse that roared'.

Rule 4: Make the enemy live up to its own book of rules

Christine used this rule in her early dealings with the NSW Police Association. The Women's Branch of the Association was fighting to expand the duties and number of women in policing without much support from the Association. By searching through the Association Rules, they found that they had to be given support for their cause. You might think that should have been obvious but in the mid 1970s it wasn't.

Another example of this rule is when businesses proclaim their ethics or corporate social responsibilities. These can be used to hold them accountable, to use their own words against them.

Rule 5: Ridicule is man's most potent weapon

The term ridicule includes mockery, derision, scorn, scoffing or contempt and, as a verb, to deride, mock, jeer at, sneer at, insult or disparage. Many people have been subjected to this rule and it can hurt the most. When Christine was nominated as the Victorian Chief Commissioner of Police, one of the Victorian newspapers characterised her as the 'Lollipop Lady from Wollongong', referring to the fact that thirty years previously she had directed traffic and pedestrians. Even though the ridicule is usually not accurate, with emotional commentary added it can leave you feeling that you have no comeback.

Those who write about this rule suggest there is no defence. But Christine's view is that there is: ignore it. Just let it go past, realise that it's meant to wound and make you stop saying or doing something. The most effective response is to not let it have that effect—to proceed anyway.

Two other pieces of advice for specifically influencing recognise the political context and dimensions of many major changes leaders are involved in: developing political smarts, and generating pressure from both within and without.

Political smarts

Influencing requires leaders to read situations, to know when a specific policy might really appeal to the current government or management. When Christine was an Assistant Commissioner in the NSW Police, she wanted to expand the number of Aboriginal community liaison officers. Funds were always an issue and lack of them was used to refuse this request. The minister asked Christine one day, 'Do you have any good ideas about how to expand the number of Aboriginal people in the police?' She promptly explained to him an initiative of appointing Aboriginal community liaison officers. He announced a new policy the following day, and Christine knew what the costs would be and had the recruitment program planned. She had been waiting for the right opportunity! Over the following years, forty new Aboriginal community liaison officers were hired.

Another, more recent example comes from her work as the Chair of Good Shepherd Microfinance. They have a strong track record of offering no-interest loans to low-income earners, but they wanted to get more political support and visibility for their services as an alternative to payday lenders, who were charging exorbitant interest. They approached the incumbent Liberal government with an idea that fitted their political philosophy, with the principle being: 'a hand up, not a handout'. The government responded positively, because what Good Shepherd were doing was consistent with the Liberal Government message.

Timing is an important component of political smarts. What else is on the agenda at the time? Are funds available? Is an election looming, or can the reforms you are seeking be seen as consistent with a broader political agenda?

Pressure from within and without

In trying to lead change in organisations, part of your focus is the internal organisation and identifying allies inside who can help lead it. But external stakeholders and allies are just as important. How can you bring about change by encouraging pressure from outside the organisation? Identify the critics of the status quo who might help you bring about change. The media played a significant role in bringing about change in Victoria and New South Wales police; for example, media attention to corruption and underworld murders in Victoria ensured a continued community focus on these very difficult issues and a desire from the government to see progress. As part of tackling gangland warfare, Victoria Police convened a day's discussion inviting all their critics, including many in the media. They asked the media what they would do to solve the problem. How would they go about doing things differently? That day and the ensuing dialogue with external commentators and experts not only resulted in great answers but converted armchair critics to being in there with the police. They had a better understanding of the issues and used their own profiles to support change, not undermine it.

Influencing and enabling from women's perspective

Interestingly, but perhaps not surprisingly, most published research and literature on influencing has been written by men, sometimes with the assumption that they've covered all the approaches and that the gender of the person working with them is irrelevant. In fact, a substantial body of research indicates differently: when women use the same approaches as men, they are perceived differently from their male counterparts.

The literature on effective negotiation provides a case in point. Advocates for more women in leadership often advise them to negotiate for a higher starting salary or increments, more resources, bigger budgets or performance bonuses. However, the research shows that women are perceived differently from men when they negotiate actively. They are more likely to be seen as greedy or ambitious and to be penalised for asking for more. One theory for why this perception occurs is that women, and especially women in leadership, are held to feminine ideals and stereotypes of looking after the team and sacrificing themselves for the greater good. Masculine stereotypes work the opposite way, where men are more likely to be rewarded for being assertive and ambitious. An analysis of 4600 people across 840 Australian workplaces confirmed that women did ask for raises but were much less likely to get them than men. The problem wasn't women's reticence but how bosses judged them.[7] What are other approaches to influencing and persuading that women especially have employed to good effect?

Use research and evidence and hold others accountable

It is surprising how rarely organisations draw on research and data to support change. But people are persuaded by it and it is motivating for others to know that actions and programs are evidence-based. Have the evidence research available so that people can see the facts of the matter or the pieces of research that might substantiate a decision.

Invoke 'borrowed protection'

Christine remembers going to a girls' secondary school and marvelling at the emphasis on science and maths and the number of senior girls opting to study these subjects, which was not the norm at the time. When she asked how the school had got so many girls studying science, the response was, 'The nuns said so!' This is an example of borrowed protection, where an external person with authority is invoked and people follow suit. Whether it is because a parent, teacher or boss 'said so', invoking borrowed protection gives legitimacy to valued courses of action.

Draw on networks

Christine has been part of interview panels in her various roles and in a recent case asked an interviewee what networks she might be able to access to help her carry out the new role. Out rolled an amazing range of experiences and contacts that would make her potential role much easier. They included a women's network, an international think tank and a role in the G20 summit. People know others through so many avenues. Women may not to want to use or exploit networks in the same way men do. This is sometimes understandable if the goal is simply personal career advancement, but if the endpoint is some greater good, like getting a valuable policy through or a reform initiative on an agenda, then a contact or relationship can facilitate this goal.

Offer and support educational and development opportunities

One of the quiet ways Christine set about influencing policing culture was to encourage and support individual employees to undertake further education and leadership development. The idea of undertaking general tertiary study, for example, a degree in social work or community leadership programs, was not part of the traditional model of police training. Encouraging police officers to join external programs meant that they would be exposed to leaders from other sectors and encouraged to think of themselves as not just police officers but having a broader community leadership role. Uniformed and non-uniformed staff were also encouraged to pursue qualifications in technical areas of policing, which meant that those participating became part of national and international networks of academics and experts.

One of the most influential things we believe a leader can do is encourage people to be exposed to wider ideas and to develop themselves. A distinction that Amanda's research has explored is between the 'banking model' of education, where students have knowledge 'owned' by teachers 'deposited' in the students, and what is sometimes termed the 'midwifery model',[8] where education helps students find out for themselves what they know, to build knowledge and confidence from their experience and to empower them to become shapers of their own learning. The power remains with the teacher in the banking model, but the midwifery model enables the learner to become a leader.

One of the inevitable consequences of encouraging people to seek broader education is that they begin to critique the systems and practices from which they came. They can become disruptive change agents, bringing consequences that must be managed personally and institutionally. This process also requires leaders and teachers to accept that we can't control the outcomes. Rather, we must have confidence that individuals will use new ideas and knowledge to make contributions in diverse ways inside and outside organisations, and our role is to be enablers and facilitators.

Be aware of and build physical presence

The evidence that our bodies and physical gestures are an important part of our presence in leadership is discussed in detail in chapter 10. Sometimes leaders, and especially women leaders, experience their bodies as an impediment to leadership: they feel they need to camouflage their physical attributes or 'tone down' the impact of their femaleness in male-dominated organisations.[9]

In the past few years, psychological research has provided solid evidence that our body state influences and changes minds. For example, the work of Harvard researcher Amy Cuddy shows that how we sit, especially in important situations like interviews, influences how confident and effective we feel and, in turn, enhances judgements about our ability and promote ability. Our bodies do this by changing the mix of hormones circulating within us, which in turn impacts our thoughts. Cuddy suggests that before important meetings or events we should experiment with 'power poses': standing up straight, putting our arms out and up, lifting out our chest.[10] Although there is evidence that there are gender differences in how these physical effects and postures are experienced and perceived, it is important to recognise that our physical selves are potentially influential to ourselves and others—positively and negatively. Especially in challenging situations, sitting or standing with a straight back, opening the chest, breathing deeply and slowing your voice can all enhance your impact and the confidence with which your message is projected and heard.

Tell stories

Research confirms that narratives and stories are very powerful vehicles through which audiences hear—and feel—others' experiences, relate them to their own opportunities and challenges, and find new ways of thinking about and acting in their own lives. In telling stories from our own experience we simultaneously enact and modify existing narratives and create new meanings and narratives in the living moment.[11] Scholars such as Harvard educationalist Howard Gardner argue that having a compelling story told well is a key element of leadership effectiveness, enabling a deeper connection with followers.

For many years, Christine has been telling stories to persuade groups to do things differently or to illuminate what they might achieve. She admits that she never really saw this as something out of the ordinary until she started to get feedback. Many people said they loved her stories; they could recognise their own dilemmas in them and new actions became possible. Stories are what people remember and what inspires them to change. Christine encourages leaders to choose stories from their own and other people's experiences that will engender a sense of optimism and confidence in the particular group or audience whom they are seeking to enable.

Sometimes people think that relating their own experiences is self-indulgent or that their experience is idiosyncratic and not relevant to others. Or that they don't have any valid leadership experience worth listening to compared to other more senior people. Yet the evidence is that even in the most hard-driving corporate environments and analytical cultures, stories are memorable and compelling facilitators of change. A good example of this is women and leadership. An enormous amount of research has now established the business case for diversity. This research shows that organisations with more diversity and women in their senior ranks do better on indicators of organisational performance, attract and retain talented employees and have lower costs in terms of training and turnover. Many people expected that simply presenting this evidence would lead to changes in organisational cultures that would make them more open and inclusive. However, the evidence is that changes are more likely to be driven by stories and personal experience; for example, by CEOs and senior leaders hearing about and telling stories of individual women being blocked from opportunities.[12] Being prepared to share stories, as opposed to data, may be the catalyst for more transformative changes.

While a lot of the research and writing about influencing assumes that any influence is good influence, key questions for us are 'why' and 'to what ends' we seek to persuade others. If we can satisfy ourselves that the value, opportunities or outcomes that will arise from such influence are good and ethical, then all the approaches and strategies we have explored here are worth experimenting with, even if they take us outside our customary ways of doing things.

7
Valuing conversations

> ... *women's stories are universal ... the sense of commonality and confidence that comes from their story telling is profound and capable of altering the course of human lives.*
>
> Quentin Bryce, 2013

Think of a conversation you've had over the last six months that didn't go as you hoped. It might have been a conversation with a manager or someone else you wanted to influence, a peer or someone who works for you. What happened? How did you feel about the way it unfolded? What did you learn from it—apart from perhaps avoiding that kind of conversation in future?

Think now about a conversation you need to have, but for one reason or another you are putting it off. It might be with a manager about an issue that is troubling you. It might feel potentially sensitive or explosive, therefore career limiting. It might be with someone who works for you who you'd like to be able to guide more effectively. It might be a conversation with a colleague or peer who you are worried won't take any notice or will take it the wrong way. Reflect on why this conversation is so hard for you. What are you telling yourself that is contributing to your procrastination?

A willingness and capacity to initiate important conversations and to listen deeply in response is a key and often underrated aspect of leadership. Modelling and influencing the quality of listening and talking around you is a powerful way to shape organisational culture, energise others to solve problems and find new paths towards collectively valued outcomes. We want to share our own learning on this and some exercises designed to inspire you to experiment with conversations. What are some of the things that get in the way of you having conversations? What strategies can be used to increase the likelihood of conversations being meaningful and fruitful for all parties?

The reality is that even if you avoid difficult conversations, they are always going on whether you like it or not. Some of these conversations include:

- those in advance of important meetings between individual members—in hallways, behind office doors or at the corner coffee shop

- the ones playing out in the minds of various players who have a strong vested interest

- 'what if' scenarios we tell ourselves about the risks of saying or doing something—how we might look stupid or get taken down a peg by others

- those between people not directly involved in or excluded from formal meetings

- the ones occurring simultaneously in the minds of participants as a meeting unfolds: 'What he is really saying is ...'

- multiple post-meeting debriefs among participants, in the minds of those affected and then in the replay later that night over dinner or on the phone with family and friends.

These multiple, sometimes contradictory conversations are always in play and potentially influential. They are one of the reasons why it is important to initiate respectful and honest conversations with those who matter to you, to speak as openly and truthfully as you can, and to hopefully leave less to hearsay, second-guessing, rumour and rumination.

Why some conversations can feel difficult

Initiating and making time for conversations is often not easy. Competing demands can push the needed conversation to the bottom of a long to-do list. We worry that we won't do a good job of the conversation, especially if the issue feels sensitive or is likely to be taken the wrong way. We may fear that the person we are speaking to will explode in anger, dissolve in tears or even make a formal complaint, and then what?

Further, organisational norms sometimes encourage either superficial—'How are you?' 'Good!' when things are definitely not—or highly directive exchanges that are not really conversations at all. In trying to initiate something different, we can feel at best vulnerable and at worst stupid. Sometimes the hesitation lies with managers who feel they must have answers or actions to offer in conversations. At the same time most hear from their staff that 'they just want to have an open conversation about the issues'. Having a conversation requires us to be present and respect the other person enough to allocate our full attention, to try and listen for what the other person needs, rather than make assumptions that we must offer a fix.

In their useful book *Difficult Conversations*, author Douglas Stone and his colleagues highlight a common myth that feelings have no place in effective conversation— that you've somehow got to banish emotions. Yet most difficult conversations are about feelings. Unless there is space and permission to at least acknowledge these in the conversation—for example, why one party is feeling misinterpreted or misjudged or overlooked—then nothing will be resolved. Their advice is to have feelings, or those feelings will have you—that is, the feelings will hold the conversation hostage, dominating implicitly and sabotaging efforts to work through, respond appropriately to or solve the issue.

Another common obstacle to having conversations in our experience is the belief that the manager or leader's job is to problem-solve. In this scenario, someone who may be experiencing difficulties at work talks to their manager. Instead of having a conversation about those difficulties, which ideally gives the person experiencing them insight into how they could see or respond differently to them, the manager jumps in with a list of actions or ways to solve the difficulty. Not all the time, but often, these are not felt by the person involved as solutions at all. Rather, they are perhaps felt as evidence the manager hasn't heard them or just wants to get them out of their office as quickly as politely possible.

Part of many managers' identities and sense of their value is as a problem-solver, a 'fixer'. It is often what individuals have been rewarded for. Yet when it comes to working through issues with others it is rarely useful. Even if an individual seeks us out, ostensibly asking for advice, it is almost always better to have ways of helping them find solutions that seem possible for them. The shift from being a problem-solver to being a coach requires recognition by the person in the position of power that this isn't about them or demonstrating their superior problem-solving skills. It involves a willingness to give something else.

How to initiate important conversations

One of the most difficult parts of leading and managing change is having conversations that you, or they, or both of you don't want to have. An example from Christine's experience is a conversation she had with a senior police officer concerning an incident that had been reported to her. The situation didn't add up. Christine decided that she needed to back her hunch and invite this senior officer into her office, even though she had been advised by the lawyers that it was now a matter for investigation and she shouldn't interfere. She sat alongside him and after preliminaries asked if there was something he needed to share with her about the circumstances. A few simple open questions and some silence allowed him the opportunity to tell Christine what had really happened.

When we work with groups on conversations we often ask them to brainstorm the features of good—productive, helpful, satisfying—conversations (see 'Features of a good conversation'). The lists they come up with usually include the same key elements: good conversations come from an intention to help or support, with the initiator being keen to learn, not judge, and there is preparedness to really listen, to give time and space to the topic under discussion. If we ask groups to tell us what a bad conversation looks like, it's the opposite. There's a high degree of consensus and it is worth reminding ourselves of it and of the value to others in conversing this way.

Features of a good conversation:
- a tone of inquiry not accusation

- language that shows you are interested

- setting and environment are appropriate—not too formal or confronting

- listening to what's not said—feelings and voice

- thinking about what also might be happening in the person's life

- coming from a good, generous place

- courage to be open

- sense of curiosity and empathy

- willingness to learn new things—'I didn't know that'—a fuller appreciation of the circumstances

- figuring out why you are having the conversation in advance

- checking back in with the person you are talking to by asking, for example, 'Is this what I heard?'

- following instincts

- being prepared but not over-prepared, and open and well-informed but not overly rehearsed or prescriptive

- not blaming or issuing judgements

- thinking about the timing—immediate or is a delay a good thing

- silence and space allowed.

Elements of good conversations

In conversations with individuals or groups, there are several elements that will determine their effectiveness for you and others involved.

Consider your intent and role

What is your intent in initiating conversations? Sometimes you want to just tell someone something you think they should know or to give them your opinion, experience or knowledge. Though well meaning, these are very rarely useful or effective intents from which to initiate a conversation. Research shows that most valuable conversations involve a shift from the intent of 'telling' to one of 'learning something new'.[1]

What does this shift—if genuine—enable? First, it gives us the opportunity to set aside your own prejudices, judgements and views and to be genuinely open to hearing the other person's experience. Even more importantly, the other person in the conversation will sense your openness, be more likely to volunteer what really matters to them and feel encouraged to come up with their own insights and ways forward, which are often the outcomes we are seeking from such a conversation.

In Christine's example above, the only way that honest exchange could have been achieved was for her to demonstrate a willingness to listen and learn. Until that point, the officer had been locked into a defensive game of covering up, causing him more and more anguish. He couldn't extricate himself without sensing the genuine intent of his commanding officer being prepared to hear the predicament from his point of view.

Reflecting on intent also opens us up to consider our role in conversations. Again, a wide range of research suggests that seeing ourselves as 'expert', the one giving orders or the holder of the truth, is rarely useful in leadership, although there may be other contexts where it is appropriate. A more valuable way to consider our role may be as an *enabler*, a container of alternative views or experiences and an opener of space for something that would otherwise not be raised. In the context of dialogue, MIT theorist William Isaacs describes leadership as the capacity to hold the container for complex sets of ideas, pressures and people as challenges arise and unfold.[2]

Part of being open to being an enabler is being prepared to let go of ego. If we are holding too tight to the idea of ourselves as the most senior, expert or experienced on a topic, then we are likely to be evaluating ourselves and others and not being truly open.[3] We need to be prepared to be seen as not having all the answers or as still learning in order to initiate good conversations.

Slow down and acknowledge emotions

One of the most common reasons conversations fail to occur is fear of emotions. People avoid conversations so they won't hurt the feelings of others or reveal their own emotions, which in both cases may seem hard to control or be potentially damaging. In leadership, there is often a lot of pressure to not show emotion, to believe that the best way forward is to suppress your own emotions and discourage others from expressing feelings.

While these are very understandable human responses, the reality is that almost all important conversations involve feelings and emotions. Unexpressed or unacknowledged feelings are usually the things holding people back from change. Recent leadership research confirms that a central part of leadership effectiveness often involves emotional sensitivity and empathy, which are the hallmarks of leading with integrity and authenticity.

In order to work with feelings:

- slow down

- breathe and pay attention to your own body and that of the other person—consciously relax your jaw, shoulders and other parts of the body that hold tension

- shift the direction from 'How can I get through this?' to 'How can I allow and trust what unfolds to be of value?'

- create a different kind of space—perhaps not in the usual place, giving some advance warning along the lines of 'I'm not sure I understand your experience and views on this. Can we take some time to help me to do this?'

- be prepared for others' feelings and the heat and tension that may arise. As Christine described when she went to announce the closure of the Armed Offenders Squad, she had to be prepared herself to be physically there 'in the belly of the beast'. She needed to demonstrate that she knew this was big, wouldn't fold under the tension and hadn't arrived at the decision without a lot of thought

- acknowledge others' feelings, be respectful without blaming, don't confuse feelings with judgements

- understand your own feelings, separate them from judgements and self-judgements and foster compassion—for yourself and others.

Listen openly, deeply and in new and different ways

On our programs, many participants are already very experienced listeners. Some have been trained in various forms of listening as professionals, coaches and mentors in clinical, teaching and social-work settings. Yet we have almost always found that inviting people to experiment and practise new forms of listening, such as listening from stillness, is highly valuable.[4] This is because all of us develop routines and habits of listening that can mean we are not truly present to *this* person, at *this* moment and to the issues they are bringing. Thus, the usual active-listening prompts may be experienced as ritualistic. We may feel we are listening but others see us as just putting on our 'nodding face'.

We also give opportunities for leaders on our programs to get feedback from an observer about how they listen and how they coach. In conversations designed to coach a speaker, what are the impacts of the coach's body language, the words they use, the interventions they adopt, the encouragement they give or solutions they suggest? Getting immediate feedback of this kind can highlight blind spots or help us see where our intentions don't get the result we are seeking.

Lead reflective dialogue

A key part of many leaders' work is shaping and participating in meetings, as either a chair or a member. These meetings include regular briefings of existing teams, sharing information among stakeholders, board meetings, and brainstorming difficult issues or innovations. Although these meetings have important differences in purpose and composition, we have found that they all benefit from certain principles, such as an atmosphere where a few voices don't dominate and all people feel heard. We've also found that it is useful to help leaders in groups see their role more broadly, as one of shaping the quality of reflective dialogue, whether or not they are the formal chair at the meeting.

What might leaders do to help groups move from polite or polarising exchanges to more meaningful interaction?[5] Again there is a consensus when we ask groups this question, which can be seen below.

Moving teams from politeness to reflective dialogue:

- share a problem, have 'skin in the game'

- use/encourage creativity

- give permission to shape rules and call behaviour

- STOP! Make your words count

- use independent facilitators or consultants, e.g. to agree on different terms of reference

- have a rotating chair

- revisit and set new ground rules

- change form of papers and prompt better preparation

- have a conversation about 'us as a team'

- build trust with 'health checks' at start

- learn each other's styles

- persist

- apply diagnostics on problem and group, explore how to fix

- give your power away

- bust myths

- have individuals take ownership of issues or problems

- call out bad behaviour

- establish shared purpose

- disclose own experiences, be prepared to be vulnerable

- use humour

- be both on the 'balcony' and the 'dance floor'.

The conversations we have as leaders matter—both the momentous ones, which involve peoples' reputations and careers, and the less planned and fleeting ones, which can equally change the course of lives, helping people to be courageous, act and make changes. Quite simply, good practices in conversation have big impacts.

8
'Hot coals' management

As a manager, you can make an enormous positive difference to someone's life—or you can stuff it up.

Christine Nixon

Christine's first encounter with good management was her mother, who seemed to be able to manage many roles: full-time in various positions at Coles Variety Stores, running a household, secretary of the Church Council, mother to two kids (often on her own), leader or 'Brown Owl' to a Brownie pack of thirty girls, among many other commitments. The only thing that used to cause her problems, Christine recalls, was not having enough money to pay the bills.

In her younger days, Christine worked at the same store as her mother. She worked as a casual on school holidays and Saturday mornings from 1968 to 1971. In another uncanny coincidence, and through her father's contacts, Amanda's first 'proper' job was in the 1970 school holidays, also at a Coles Variety Store. Both of us had the opportunity of observing and learning about good and bad managers through these early experiences. What are the qualities of good managers—those who you might walk over hot coals for?

This kind of management is different from leadership but is very important in its impact.

Christine recalls that management has fascinated her through much of her working life, starting with Coles and the local chemist, in the NSW Police and in her various roles in the forty years since. She thinks she has seen the whole spectrum of managers—the good, the bad and the dangerous. She's also been responsible for managing thousands of managers, and has been a participant, victim, practitioner and observer. She says:

> We had two types of managers in the Manly Coles store. There were the women called floorwalkers. They solved all the key problems, made sure all the stock orders were in, collected the money at the end of the day and checked it, and assisted with staff training and mentoring. They worked closely with the other managers, the male store manager (who we saw infrequently) and the male trainee assistant managers. A few other males were employed as stock and warehouse men, or worked on counters.
>
> I worked mostly on one of the counters and in the office and had an idea that at the end of my schooling I might join the trainee management program. I was quickly discouraged from this idea when I was told that they didn't have women in the management program. How could I have not noticed that?
>
> As a young police officer beginning at the bottom of the ladder in the NSW Police, I also saw a great variety of managers. In my first roles, including in the School Lecturing Section, one thing was common: most of the sergeants were men. They seemed to have worked out that we women did the work (lectured children and directed traffic), and they, the managers, checked up on us, drove the only available cars, made appointments for us to work and seemed to quite enjoy their Monday to Friday jobs.
>
> After having studied management, I became more disillusioned with most of the managers I worked for. I remember asking then Inspector John Avery, who later became NSW Police Commissioner, how he described good management. His answer was, 'Think about the managers you would walk over hot coals

for. Look at the qualities of good managers you've had. Follow what they do.'

My only trouble was I didn't have a lot of managers that fitted that hot coals category. Thus began for me a search to hear from others what they valued in managers and to find out whether good managers were as rare for them as they had been for me.

Management and leadership

While most of this book is about leadership, management is very important too. Both need to be done well to create great workplaces and effective organisations. American management guru Peter Drucker is quoted as saying, 'Management is doing things right. Leadership is doing the right things.' This captures the idea that good management includes understanding and implementing procedures and policies that advance the goals of the organisation. It includes planning, policy development, organising, developing and implementing controls, creating systems, and deploying and monitoring resources. Drucker provides a lot of valuable common sense about managing, including pointing out that there is nothing quite so useless as doing with great efficiency something that should not be done at all.

Another way that leadership and management are differentiated is to recognise that management involves efficiently and effectively running existing systems, whereas leadership involves change and a preparedness to disturb and disrupt the status quo. As an example, in a widely cited article called 'What Leaders Really Do', leadership scholar John Kotter says that managers 'maintain control, while leaders take charge of "change". Both are required in order for organizations to flourish'.[1]

Drawing on these distinctions, it is likely that management and leadership require different skill sets and, some say, personality types.[2] Yet our argument is that good management is not a mystery, nor is it rocket science. It requires not stellar intelligence or extraordinary cognitive skills but a simple commitment to treat others as valuable human beings.

Managers you would walk over hot coals for

Christine describes a number of managers who she would walk over hot coals for:

> One got me out of trouble when I was a young constable at Darlinghurst Police Station, helping me catch up on a backlog of work that had been overwhelming me. He wrote to me when I became the Police Commissioner and suggested that he had helped get me into that position, and he was right. Another very good manager used to send me to meetings on his behalf so I could get experience interacting with a range of other government and community organisations. Another manager really helped me understand my role and guided me through various scenarios so I'd be able to keep out of trouble. Another had enough faith in me and threw me in the deep end, knowing that I would learn to swim that way.

Following this interest in the qualities of good managers, Christine now regularly asks two simple questions during her teaching and programs:

1. How many managers have you had that you would walk over hot coals for?

2. What were the qualities of these managers that you really valued?

The responses are incredibly consistent across now over 14,000 people. Whether bankers, Defence Force personnel, people working in police, corrections and not-for-profit organisations, nurses, health professionals, electricians, construction workers, transport professionals, railway staff, teachers, or professional and occupational groups, they all report similar numbers and the same qualities they value in managers. In almost every group there are always one or two participants who've had no managers who have inspired or helped them enough to walk over hot coals for them. There is often a significant group who've only had one, sometimes as many as 16 per cent of the group. The number who have had four or five managers they'd walk over hot coals for is rarely more than 4 per cent of the group.

You might be shocked that people can work for so many years and come across so few managers they would go the extra mile for, but the evidence certainly fits with Christine's experience and, obviously, that of many others. Participants are also surprised when they look around and find they are just like most others in their responses. The lucky few who've had several are surprised to find how unusual their experience is.

Turning to the question of the qualities and behaviours of hot-coals managers, again, different groups show remarkable similarities. As an example, one group from Sydney in 2015 chose the following qualities:

- transparent, positive, accessible and open

- shared information, not tricky, didn't use code to exclude me

- listened—took the time to hear me, offered me the chance to talk

- supportive and gave me opportunities to try a new job, to act on behalf of the boss

- encouraged me to have a go, to take on a new task or apply for a new role

- reliable and organised

- trusted me and had faith in me—gave me the task and let me get on with it

- empowered me, challenged me to do better—saw I had the skills to do the task or job even when I was not so sure

- had my back, and when things went wrong protected me

- valued me and took the time to understand where I was coming from

- treated me as a human being and made me feel my efforts were valuable

- inspired me—made me feel that I could do anything, that I was part of the bigger picture and something very important

- had a sense of humour

- acted in accordance with their own values—held themselves accountable and behaved consistently

- cared about how I was going, my wellbeing

- said good morning, asked how things were going and listened to my responses.

Other groups volunteered very similar qualities and behaviours. For instance, a group of women leaders in Adelaide suggested hot-coals managers were 'authentic, understood my strengths and developed me, were supportive, inclusive, wise and said "thank you".' A Melbourne group of women added, 'Saw my potential, calm, positive, decisive, had my back, outward focus, confident, and advocated for me.'

When John Avery asked Christine to think about hot coals managers, he also asked her, as she asks participants now after considering the second question, 'So is that the way you manage?' And that's the real point of this exercise—because managers can make an enormous difference in people's lives. They can hinder or add to success.

What forms does this good management take? As one example, Christine heard a police officer on radio complain that no one from the police human resources department came to visit him while he was hospitalised. While this is an understandable request, Christine maintains it isn't the responsibility of human resources to follow up; it is the responsibility of managers. They should have been the ones visiting, to make sure that he was okay. Did he need any help getting to the doctor for appointments? Were there other ways they could support him? When Christine was Chief Commissioner in Victoria, she adopted this practice, which she learned from another CEO. When people are sick or have been injured at work, send them a card wishing them well and hoping for a speedy recovery. The impact is important and a survey conducted by Victoria Police's insurance agency confirmed that police members nominated this strategy as significant.

In another instance, a police officer collapsed at work and was in a coma in hospital. Christine made arrangements to meet his wife at the hospital to talk to her about how her husband was going. Christine arrived and was advised by the nurses that the wife wasn't coming. The nurses suggested she could sit with the officer for a while and chat, and so she did. She had had a bad week and decided to tell her colleague in the coma all about it. The nurses passed by occasionally, amused at her chatting to an unconscious and very ill person, and brought her a cup of tea.

The police officer recovered and some months later came to see Christine to thank her for the support he had been given by his managers and for her visit. She asked him whether he remembered anything she had said to him. He said no, and Christine was pretty glad about that. She told him he was one of the best listeners she's ever had.

Christine's favourite qualities in a hot coal manager

- care

- respect me and others

- articulate and aspire to goals

- are accountable

- provide both pressure and support

- stretch me and others in the organisation further than they think possible

- are authentic

- share themselves and their wisdom

- admit to mistakes

- don't take themselves too seriously

- put things in perspective.

Why care about managing?

Sometimes in textbooks and research, management and leadership get mythologised as high ideals that we feel we can't deliver on. Many organisations have complex performance management systems with rankings for management behaviours. While these systems are sometimes helpful, we need to remind ourselves that it isn't hard to be a good manager who makes a big difference to others. What Christine's surveys show is that there is a clear consensus on the managerial behaviours and qualities that make a positive difference to those working with and below them. Simple genuine gestures, offered in the moment rather than scheduled, are what matter. A manager's role is to notice the other person, see their potential value and give priority and time to them.

While leadership has been the focus of much more research and writing in recent decades and is what we are primarily concerned with here, good management should not be devalued.[3] They work hand in hand. We want to remind everyone working with and alongside others—those with management positions and titles and those without—that taking time to respect, listen, encourage and occasionally protect others at work is valuable to those who experience it as well as to the organisations of which they are a part.

Part 3

FLOURISHING

Now we turn to how to flourish in leadership. While achieving what you set out to do and pursuing valuable purposes is pivotal, so too is doing it in a way that is sustainable and satisfying. This is what we mean by flourishing.

Our focus moves to you as leader or aspiring leader. What matters to you? What is non-negotiable? Where will you draw the line? In our experience these lines vary for individuals but you need to turn the gaze back on yourself and be open to reflection and exploration, recalibration and (re)discovery.

This process of being prepared to focus on yourself is important for several reasons. The first is the evidence that while organisations are hard to change, people can and do. If you are interested in leading change in organisations, you must inevitably focus on supporting people to make changes, including for yourself. There is case study after case study in organisational change research that documents how changing structures, technologies, reporting lines, processes, brands and/or marketing strategies often produces little real change. Models of how leaders should 'manage change' often act as if the leader is somehow above the action, orchestrating change. Yet leaders can't expect their teams to embrace the unknown unless at some level the leaders don't also demonstrate their own willingness to be open and adapt to what unfolds. Humans are extraordinarily good at looking like they've made adaptations but, inside, are holding on very tight to what is familiar, even if it's not viable any more.

A second reason is the further evidence about the limited impact leaders often have. Organisational life is dynamic, with changes that are uncontrollable by single individuals, even charismatic leaders held up as gurus of change and innovation. Mostly, organisations don't behave predictably or even rationally. While change is inevitably messy, the good news for leaders is that modest actions can have big impacts, that everyday interactions can be as influential as the big strategies or marketing plans. This evidence encourages leaders to be humble, but also persistent and purposeful.

The third reason to turn the focus on you is the most important from our perspective. Leadership is not about getting through the work. To do leadership well, it needs to be part of your growth and development, providing pleasure, fulfilment and new possibilities for you. In our work with women on our programs, it is this possibility that is most pressing for the participants. Many leaders have the technical skills to do their jobs. Where they need most help is in how to focus their efforts and energies, how to not get caught up in the wrong things, and how to say 'no' or ask for help when they are overloaded. They need help to find the good parts of their role, and to stop, relish and celebrate these with their teams and colleagues rather than rushing to the next task.

In our experience, women leaders often need support to value themselves and their wellbeing enough to make radical changes, to say, 'I've done what I can here', to resign from intolerable roles, to let go of senior positions and golden handcuffs, to start again doing something completely different. One of the best parts of our work has been hearing from women who have—at least partially because of our work together and the collegiality and support of other women—made big, satisfying changes in their leadership work.

9
Power: How to find it, use it and own it

> *Women need power to change things ... Participation is the start, but power is the end.*
>
> Julia Gillard, 2016

Women seeking to exercise leadership have often felt ambivalent about power—and for good reason. Power as a concept can bring with it the implication of coercion, of 'lording' it over others—notice the gender in that figure of speech—and as the abuse and misuse of authority. For millennia, and still in contemporary societies, women have been victims of power in family, religious, educational and workplace contexts. Yet there are many reasons why anyone interested in effective leadership should also be interested in supplementing sources of authority, such as decision-making responsibilities, with other sources of power.

Informal sources of power can include such things as individual track record, credibility, expertise, empathy and emotional intelligence, charisma, fortitude and courage, an appetite for risk, and creating new ideas and opportunities. Sources of power also include relationships, communities, history and networks, women's traditions and cultural wisdom. They might include, as they do in many Indigenous communities, cultural and spiritual knowledge, and a licence bestowed by the community to pass on cherished traditions that are embodied or oral in their wisdom. As an example, some research in which Amanda was involved showed how the traditions and practices of midwifery have long provided powerful models of leadership in Indigenous communities. This source of power is intergenerational and collaboratively created with grandmothers, mothers and other women who understand the importance of empowering and supporting women in childbirth.[1]

Power, like leadership, is one of those important ideas that has often been defined in masculine terms, reflecting male experiences. In leadership studies, explorations of power have similarly overfocused on male experience and writers have been predominantly white men.[2] In the area of power, as in leadership, what women have to say about their experiences gaining, exercising and deploying power has been neglected. Ways of thinking about power—what it is, who has it and how it should be used—have historically often simply made women feel powerless and marginalised, or fearful of using power in ways that mimic oppressors.

To remedy this situation, we suggest several approaches. First, we need to pay renewed attention to women writers—feminists, activists, academics, philosophers and leaders—who are rethinking the nature of power and power in leadership. Speaking at the 1994 Beijing International Women's Conference, American feminist and politician Bella Abzug expressed this as the confident expectation that women would change the nature of power rather than power changing women. Victoria's first woman Premier, Joan Kirner, and commentator Moira Rayner, both pioneers in fostering women's political activism, wrote *The Women's Power Handbook* precisely in order to guide women to be confident in acquiring and exercising power.

A second approach is to listen to and learn from women as they talk about what sources of power they draw on, how they supplement formal authority, and how they support others to step up and advocate for shared goals. Drawing on some of the programs we have taught and our separate work, we identify the experiences that women leaders encounter that can, in the moment, make them feel powerless again. We examine some external circumstances that women leaders face and can prompt feelings of powerlessness, such as the unexpected withdrawal of support or, worse, sabotage by other senior women, and the pervasive problem of backlash—that is, women with legitimate authority being subject to undermining on the basis that it was their gender, not their ability or eligibility, that got them to leadership. We share some strategies for responding to these often unexpected or seemingly non-combatable efforts to dilute someone's power. As well as external factors, we also look at internally generated doubts and fears such as the well-researched 'impostor syndrome'—more on this later.

Our intent is to help women to get better acquainted with power and to explore how to use their power towards shaping ends they, their organisations and communities value.

New conceptions of power

Our understanding of what power is and how it may be exercised has changed radically over the past fifty years.[3] Newer conceptions of power are often helpful for those who've traditionally been or felt themselves to be in powerless positions.

Power can be represented as the proverbial iceberg. The overt exercise of power by one individual over another is the visible part, above the waterline. It may involve observable direction or coercion, with a clear perpetrator and 'victim'. New views of power argue that its more important expression may be below the waterline. These power dynamics are less visible, without obvious expression. We can feel this power at play but it doesn't have to be evident in the things that are said and done between individuals. This power resides in unquestioned norms and assumptions that control what gets discussed by whom, what comes up for debate and what is left as unquestioned reality or truth. It is this larger body of power interrelationships that determines what happens in organisational contexts for good or ill.

This understanding of power helps us see more clearly how histories, legends, procedures, structures and systems become interlocking webs of power without requiring overt coercion by anyone.

However, it also enables recognition that there is power potentially in many micro acts and behaviours. There is power in resistance, in speaking out, in doing leadership differently. There is power in humour, in dissent, in proposing radical alternatives, in pointing out something others have missed or are too polite to say, in being creative or audacious. As many women's movements around the world have shown, there is power in joining and organising across class, cultural and religious grounds.

From the pioneering organisational scholar Mary Parker Follett to many contemporary women philosophers and thinkers, women have often argued for new notions of power that recognise community or collectively expressed power. In 1942 Follett first made the important distinction between 'power-over' and 'power-with', a distinction that has been picked up by numerous later theorists of power. For Follett, power-with is a collective property: a function of relationships of reciprocity between members of a group. Philosopher Hannah Arendt, in her 1970 book *On Violence*, defined power as 'the human ability not just to act but to act in concert'. The theme of power as empowerment has been prominent in the work of women who have written about power. Nancy Hartsock, for example, argues for a feminist standpoint that critiques masculine notions of power as domination and repression. She proposes a view of power that points in more 'liberatory directions'.[4]

Research by several leadership and social change scholars helps us to see that power is not intrinsically bad. Kennedy School academic Ron Heifetz and his colleagues have highlighted that a person's formal authority—the authority bestowed on leaders by boards or by governing bodies—is rarely sufficient to do the work that needs to be done in leadership. That formal authority almost always needs to be supplemented by other sources of informal power and influence. Similarly, social change activist and advocate Adam Kahane draws on the words of Martin Luther King to argue that for positive social change to occur, you need individuals exercising both power—the drive to self-realisation, as he defines it—and love, the desire for connection and belonging.[5] The two 'drives' go hand in hand, according to Kahane, with power ensuring that love is purposeful, and love ensuring that the exercise of power is generative and regenerative.

In our programs, we have learned a lot about power—not having it and finding it—from asking groups of women several questions:[6]

- What makes you feel powerless?

- What sources of power do you draw on in your leadership work?

- What has helped you find power?

- How can you own the power you do have?

Feeling powerless

The experience of powerlessness often has both a subjective and objective component. This can be seen in the list of factors that one group of women said contributed to making them feeling powerless:

- being dismissed or ignored

- asymmetrical knowledge

- not being listened to

- people overusing jargon, or running an agenda

- no support

- being bullied or cut off in meetings

- external pressures that provide us no options—for example, being financially responsible for mortgages, intensive parent or childcare responsibilities

- overbearing, dominant individuals.

In our experience, talking in our groups about the circumstances that make women feel powerless has benefit. First, the women come to understand that they are not alone. Feelings of powerlessness are widely experienced—they don't reflect individual failure and shouldn't be cause for self-blame or shame. Second, and relatedly, women understand that such dynamics as not being listened to or bullying are, sadly, common in groups and organisations. Newcomers, outsiders or those who look different are almost inevitably made to feel 'weird' or as if they are troublemakers when they raise issues others are ignoring.

Such dynamics are often just the inevitable ways groups preserve the status quo. But stepping back and understanding these dynamics gives you power! Recognising organisational dynamics for what they are helps you decide how they are going to impact you, how much attention to pay to them and whether you should, or can, learn from them.

Two particular experiences of powerlessness are worth exploring in more depth as they often come up in groups of women. The first is the 'impostor syndrome' or 'impostorism': the belief that you have achieved a position of responsibility by luck, that expectations are high and that you will be 'found out', revealed to be a fraud or inadequate. The second is when women don't feel supported by more senior women; rather, those women actively sabotage female juniors or colleagues.

Feelings of being an impostor can be fostered by a mixture of very high expectations of yourself within an organisational culture that is competitive, and does not tolerate failure but puts women in highly visible or 'token' situations where a lot seems to ride on success.[7] These combined external and subjective circumstances can elicit feelings of anxiety, lack of confidence and self-doubt. Recognising these dynamics, individuals can be supported to make a choice. One route includes continuing to react to high expectations and scrutiny by overpreparing or procrastinating, then following successful accomplishment discounting and devaluing it as luck or a 'one-off'. This then prompts you to take on more work in an effort to prove your value. Perfectionism and judgementalism are companions on this slippery vicious cycle (see Figure 9.1).

Figure 9.1: Common circumstances and responses in the impostor cycle

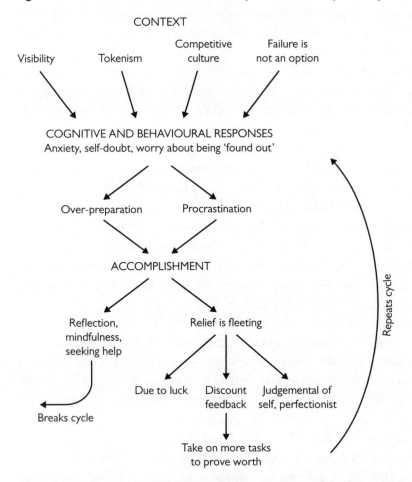

A better route is mediated by the capacity to reflect and exercise self-insight (see chapter 13), to be courageous and take calculated risks (see chapter 12), and to gain reality-checking feedback from a coach or friend. Research shows that, indeed, many of the ingredients that contribute to the cycle are available for conscious modification and learning. Excessive expectations, harsh self-judgement and preoccupation with the unbearable costs of failure are all tendencies we can notice, own and modify with reflection and mindfulness (see chapter 13). In addition, lack of skills, knowledge and support can be addressed with practical and behavioural responses, such as asking for help.

All of these strategies are helpful in interrupting and rerouting the negative cycle of feeling like an impostor. This particular category of feeling powerless shows that though circumstances may be difficult or hostile, we usually have a choice in what we make of them. It is true that women leaders are often elevated to power when the risks of failure are high. This is known as 'the glass cliff', the situation where, for example, women are asked to lead political parties into unwinnable elections. The choice comes in how women leaders then read the situation—whether they accept and embrace impossibly high expectations and discount incremental positive feedback, or whether they step back and respond selectively and realistically to the scale of the challenge.

The second experience of powerlessness volunteered by women, when other more senior women don't support and sometimes actively sabotage them, can hit very hard. It's reasonable for women to expect a 'sisterly' response, a helping hand up or at least a sounding board, in workplaces where there are few women. It doesn't always happen, and when it doesn't, it feels like betrayal.

What does sometimes occur in this situation is that women's lack of support for other women gets blown up and focused on, as if it's the dominant dynamic between women in workplaces—the 'Queen Bee syndrome'. The headline of an article in *The Telegraph* by John Bingham, reporting research on competitive behaviour across gender, blared: 'The Sisterhood Ceiling: How the final barrier to women reaching the top is ... other women'.[8] An accompanying photo showed two women arguing—though in evening dress, so it was unlikely they were in the office. The research this article reported was a well-conducted exploration showing that female participants perceived competition with same-gender co-workers as less desirable than competition with opposite-gender co-workers. Women suffered more from a highly competitive culture and experienced more 'relational damage' when working with other, very competitive women.

While the researchers were careful to point out that their work did not confirm caricatures about women having workplace catfights—in fact, the reverse—it was written up in the media in a way that concluded women's relationships with other women were the problem. Women were 'overreacting' to competitive workplace cultures and took 'too personally' highly competitive behaviour in other women. Rather than see the dog-eat-dog workplace culture as the likely problem here, the article reinforced that it was women who were the problem, and the reason why other women don't make it to the top.

In our own work with groups of women we have found it is important to:

- recognise there will be instances where women aren't supported by other women and acknowledge the impact of this on women who expect something more

- understand why such behaviour might occur; for example, it is more likely where women have been socialised into a culture of individualism and competition where no one deserves, or benefits from, special status; or if they have routinely been expected to mentor or carry on their shoulders the 'problem' of retaining women in addition to their substantial other responsibilities

- identify the problems with double standards; for example, of allowing that when men exhibit excessively competitive behaviour it's just 'what men do', while when women exhibit similar behaviours they are judged to be ruthless; or in another common example of double standards, not expecting any special support from senior men but holding women to a higher standard of nurturance, selflessness or sponsorship

- discourage women from generalising this lack of support to all senior women—the Queen Bee is a powerful idea that has traction in organisations and works against equality and opportunity, but women should not collude with cultures that readily label senior women 'bitches' or ruthless when they are simply reproducing dominant behaviours that are seen as unproblematic in men[9]

- encourage women to be supportive role models for the women around and below them. Sometimes this possibility is made all the more real because women directly experience in a leadership program the benefits of the support of other women.

Common obstacles to finding or rediscovering one's power have a lot to do with how we see ourselves and our options, in addition to external circumstances. These are:

- believing that power can only come with position

- feelings of isolation, of difference, or of being marginalised, which can produce paralysis or delay; for example, self-talk like 'I'll just fit in and wait till I understand and am more secure in the system before I act'

- waiting for someone else to authorise us

- overestimating the personal and professional risks in being powerful; for example, the narrative that goes, 'I'll get penalised/they won't talk to me/I'll get labelled a troublemaker if I speak up on this'.

Finding power and sources of power

In the context of overcoming significant personal and institutional obstacles, we have found that listening to women leaders talk about how they supplement their sources of power provides rich, diverse and valuable insights. A group of New Zealand public managers were asked about the sources of power they draw on and their answers reflect themes that are, in our experience, common among women:

- calm, peace, happiness
- networks
- saying 'no'
- reputation

- family
- gut feeling
- knowledge
- acknowledgement by others
- energy defined broadly
- other stakeholders
- data, research, facts
- respect, trust
- health and wellbeing
- sleep
- confidence that I have what I need
- a backing team in place
- flow, clarity
- adrenaline
- celebrating success
- a sense it's a 'just right' challenge now.

Other groups of women emphasise many of the same sources but also find power through place, such as their natural environment and land, and through collectively held wisdom. For example, groups of Indigenous women see power in being 'on country' or 'going bush', in discussions and seeking the wisdom of elders and aunties, and in seeking out and enacting through rituals such as dance, cultural knowledge about land, the Dreaming and ancestors. These groups often have a more embodied understanding of their own power that is tied to intergenerational wisdom, bestowed through belonging to an ancient culture.

Some strategies for finding power in the day-to-day of leadership volunteered by some of the women in our groups are:

- having an awareness of what's going on
- being in networks
- using and being an 'angel' or supporter
- finding a mentor, sponsor, cheerleader

- calling people on their actions and what they say
- recognising other people's behaviour is theirs, not yours
- identifying role models and emulating them
- initiating conversations about important issues and seeking views of people outside work, such as family members and older people who've had a lot of life experience
- putting pressure on, using media
- using your own difference
- having a prepared 'comeback'
- being authentic
- having a supportive partner
- not allowing yourself to be stereotyped
- knowing the skills you bring, recognising your own potential
- modelling behaviours you're seeking in others
- creating a soft place for others to land
- admitting mistakes
- asking for help.

In her influential 2013 book *Lean In*, Facebook's Chief Operating Officer, Sheryl Sandberg, provides a compelling diagnosis of obstacles continuing to face women in leadership:

- the stereotypes that judge a successful woman as less likeable and appealing as a colleague; for example, the Howard and Heidi curriculum vitae test, where identical CVs are judged differently depending on whether the recruiters believe the candidate is a man or a woman

- socialisation processes that teach women to attribute their success to others or good luck, to not see themselves as leaders, to not take a seat at the table.

Sandberg argues that in response women should 'lean in'; that is, they should notice when their socialisation kicks in and override it. For example, they should:

- address the 'ambition gap', and negotiate for pay and promotion

- avoid internalising failure or attributing their own success to luck or others—in Sandberg's words 'un-distort the distortion of socialisation'

- not wait for a mentor, and stop wanting to be liked

- 'fake it till you feel it' and 'fake it till you become it'.

These are all strategies for taking power and there is evidence that since *Lean In*'s publication women are demanding a better deal and pushing back on cultural norms that denigrate women; for example, women in China have been documented as resisting the 'leftover women' label and pressures to marry.

There is greater consciousness of the damage caused by labelling women and girls as 'bossy' and 'aggressive' when they are being necessarily assertive. There is also evidence of individual men acknowledging their bias and engaging in dialogue about gender. However, these actions are largely limited to individuals. There is no evidence of the sought-after structural or organisation-wide change. As we discussed in chapter 3, on many measures of equality—for example, reducing the pay gap between women and men, or increasing the numbers of women in senior corporate roles—there has been no evidence of improvement and some indicators even show an erosion of equality. In a substantial US research study of 5000 working engineers entitled 'Leaning in, but Getting Pushed Back (and Out)', Fouad and her colleagues find—yet again—that no amount of leaning in by women results in equal opportunities for women in engineering. It is the workplace culture and climate that determines whether women persist.[10] Similarly, Australian data on women in engineering show that women make up around a quarter of those who complete engineering university degrees, but only about 15 per cent stay in engineering. Because of the culture, hours regarded as necessary and lack of flexibility, many seek careers in other fields and the value of their talent and training is lost to the profession.

In her 2016 book *Lean Out*, journalist Dawn Foster suggests that Sandberg's remedy overemphasises celebrating individual success stories at the cost of addressing collectively experienced serious social inequality. Foster advocates a different set of powerful strategies:

> Fighting for equality is often misunderstood as simply being offered the same terms as men on paper. In many ways, we already have that. What we don't have is emancipation: the opportunity to be free of social and external shackles that perpetuate inequality and women's lower position. Women around the world are now demanding more: paid work, a life for their children, but also the right to be listened to, a political voice, direct democracy, and the right to a full civic life. That isn't won by keeping quiet: it's won by physically and psychologically going on strike, by shouting back, and leaning out.

Exercising and owning power through organising, collaborating and activism

There are two additional ideas for working with power that we believe may be especially valuable for women. The first is the recognition that we all do have power—however powerless we can sometimes feel—and that it is important to ensure we deploy it towards outcomes that we value. The second is the recognition that individual power can be supplemented by collective action, by joining forces with other women and men across organisational, cultural, economic, community and other boundaries, and by networking and appealing to issues that women care about.

In terms of owning power, participants on our programs volunteer the importance of giving themselves permission to direct others and to share power. Amanda remembers key events where, despite feeling marginalised and ineffectual in her immediate work context, she was reminded by others that she did have, and always does have, power. In one example, commencing a collaborative research project on Indigenous leadership with Lillian Holt, a former Director of the Centre for Indigenous Education at the University of Melbourne, Lillian suggested that Amanda start by recognising the power and privilege that come with her whiteness. As a white, educated woman, it was important for her to recognise not just that power but also the responsibility that came with it to use that power to redress injustices, speak out and act to change the status quo.

A related idea is that while our formal power can feel very constrained within our immediate organisational context, a key way to act for change is to seek alliances and partners beyond organisational borders or in the wider community. Christine's earlier example of wanting to do more on domestic violence while at Victoria Police started with approaching female ministers and heads of department to have more impact. She recognised that solitary efforts by police wouldn't succeed; there needed to be a concerted effort across the courts, social work and family services, agencies supporting women in crisis and refuges, and community and women's groups.

Jen de Vries, an academic and consulting colleague of ours who specialises in gender in leadership, introduces leaders to what she terms a 'bi-focal' or 'tri-focal' lens to help remedy gender inequality. She argues for the need to look beyond individual experiences of inequality to explore the systemic and structural barriers (bi-focal), and further adopts a view that identifies how community and societal barriers are enacted in often-invisible norms and practices that are seen as 'just the way things are' (tri-focal). De Vries and her colleague Tim Muirhead have developed a process by which men and women working together can collectively identify what they can do as individuals, and as men and women, to work for change. The following table was the result of one workshop led by de Vries and Muirhead at the University of Western Australia. They maintain that this kind of statement is always a work-in-progress, and that the work of putting it together may be as important as the list itself in helping people take responsibility for working for big societal change, and taking smaller but vital leadership actions.

Women's work	Men's work
Talk to men, leaders and each other about gender issues—keep bringing them up.	Articulate benefits for all of improved diversity.
Do leadership differently, and don't be constrained by the models of leadership you see around you.	Champion different (less 'masculine') models of leadership—be more open, communicative, compassionate and equitable.
Strive to ensure that having women in leadership leads to better workplaces (not just to women leading in 'masculine' ways).	Speak out against males' 'dominating' behaviours when you see them.
'Lean in' at work (or 'step up'). 'Lean out' at home.	'Lean out' at work (make 'space at the table'). 'Lean in' at home.
Explore challenges for women, don't minimise their impact, and support women to be gender aware.	Explore challenges for men and dialogue about male identity.
Challenge cultural assumptions about femininity at work (for example, that women lack ambition or are not serious about careers).	Challenge cultural assumptions and stereotypes about masculinity at work (for example, success at all costs).

Women's work	Men's work
Recognise that 'family-friendly' work practices should benefit men as well as women.	Fight for a more 'family-friendly' and 'person-friendly' workplace, for your own benefit.
Support men and women who need time off for family.	Demonstrate that people have wider responsibilities, including family. Use flexible polices, consider part-time work.
Resist the 'domestic' duties in the office. Say no more often. Speak up and take risks.	Identify and model gender-positive behaviour (for example, do the 'domestic' duties in the office, take the notes, listen more often and speak less often).
Stop feeling guilty about quotas and targets	Mentor and sponsor women, and ask, 'Where are the women?'

© Jen de Vries and Tim Muirhead, 2014

As an example of owning power, Amanda recently led a day workshop with academic women at a university during which the Vice Chancellor came and addressed the group. As preparation for the VC's visit, Amanda encouraged the group to be courageous and convey the career and promotion obstacles many were facing, even though several of the women confessed to feeling cynical and powerless. The Vice Chancellor went away impressed with the group and had a discussion about gender-based obstacles with deans of faculties that afternoon, and significant changes and promotions were experienced over the following months. We do have power.

10

Physicality: How women are seen as leaders and how they can respond

> *... female leaders tend to suffer a peculiarly malevolent scrutiny in the visual construction and destruction of their leadership.*
>
> Smolovic-Jones and Jackson, 2015

Tracey Spicer is one of the few broadcasters and journalists who seek to expose the pressures on women in high-profile media positions to maintain their bodies to narrow, idealised prescriptions. In recent years, she has joined other women in the spotlight to speak out about these pressures and the impact on herself and other women. In her TEDx talk, 'The Lady Stripped Bare', Spicer describes the kinds of comments she routinely encounters from bosses—that she is too 'porky' and 'too long in the tooth' to continue to front news programs.[1] Spicer uses the duration of her talk to 'physically deconstruct' her usual self-presentation, removing her make-up, heels, blow-dried hair, 'shaping' underwear, and so on. Spicer not only makes a stirring call to name and resist 'excessive grooming' pressures, but also shares the freedom and authenticity of her ungroomed self with the audience. Her voice changes and her body relaxes as she helps other women be comfortable with who they are.

In a well-publicised—but more problematic—effort to expose double standards, Australian television host Karl Stefanovic wore the same suit for a year. His co-host, Lisa Wilkinson, had earlier used the opportunity of a public awards speech to raise awareness of the pressures on women and their appearance and Stefanovic decided to run his own experiment and see if anyone noticed or if he came under pressure to change.[2] He did not—there were zero comments or complaints. He maintained, 'I'm judged on my interviews, my appalling sense of humour—on how I do my job, basically. Whereas women are quite often judged on what they're wearing or how their hair is ... that's [what I wanted to test].'[3]

Stefanovic's efforts gained publicity and plaudits from many men and women, showing that such stands can win general appeal—though some noted that while he was popular and lauded for wearing the same suit, women trying to make the same point often experience a more hostile response. Nevertheless, these examples illustrate that there is now wide recognition that men and women in public roles are judged by different standards. We want to show that there are opportunities for women and men to resist, rather than just go along with these sexist double standards around appearance, especially when you are in a position of leadership.

Our first point is that women in leadership roles experience high visibility and scrutiny, especially of their bodies, and this scrutiny is often used to cast doubt on or undermine the quality of their leadership. An example of this was the media grilling Christine received during the Bushfires Royal Commission, when she admitted going out to eat dinner during the emergency. The episode was analysed by Moira Rayner, a barrister and writer, former Equal Opportunity and HREOC Commissioner, and principal of Moira Rayner and Associates:[4]

> What did then-Commissioner Nixon do? On a day she was not rostered for duty she went into the emergency centre to contribute to fire-fighting management, worked in her office for a bit over an hour, returned to the centre, made arrangements for some briefings to ministers, and nicked off for tea.

For reasons best known to counsel assisting the Royal Commission, Nixon was cross-examined on her 'need' to leave at 6.00pm—before the insanely out-of-control firestorm status was known—and replied she had no such need. Hostile questioning from journalists after the public hearing had her admit the terrible truth: she hadn't cooked tea at home but slipped into a nearby pub with her husband and two friends for about an hour.

Did (dog-whistle: overweight and middle-aged) Commissioner Nixon get pissed? No. Did she party? Evidently not: the meal took about an hour. Did she take the rest of the night off? No: she kept in touch from home. Had she shrugged off responsibility as police commissioner for responding to the firestorm? Well, no.

Should she have waited another hour to listen to the ministerial briefing, knowing by that stage that deaths were likely? Why? What benefit, even in hindsight, would have been to hang about looking concerned, when there was nothing more she could possibly do? The full horror was not to be known until light on the following day.

The Royal Commission can't even begin to pin blame on Nixon for the widespread failure to predict the savagery of the firestorms, to save more people, or create or mend failed radio/telecommunications—all of this was in others' hands.

Nixon's only 'mistake' was to say that she 'could have done better' on Black Saturday. Everyone could have.

No man would have said this. Linguistics Professor Deborah Tannen's research into the communication patterns of women and men (*Talking From 9 to 5*) proved that even at work men communicate as they have been socialised as boys, to build up status and social credit in the hierarchy they learned in the playground. Women aim to establish relationships and commonalities, an approach that they, too, learned among their peers.

Interrogated by a woman, even a tough, sometimes ruthless manager of operational police officers could slip into a reflective acknowledgment of fallibility.

Perhaps Nixon was unnecessarily honest, too, in telling a journo where she had eaten that night, because women leaders' vulnerabilities make airborne news, and politicians who sniff the wind (better than the CFA did that horror night) will run before it.

The tongue is a little instrument, Commissioner, which does much harm. The Secretary of the Police Association—at war with the first woman Chief Commissioner of Police and first commissioner who would neither accept nor turn a blind eye to bullying—was quick to strike more matches. Opposition politicians in an election year struck poses and opened their mouths to add more fuel. Blame splashed around, but not from all of the bushfire-affected survivors (notably, not from Kinglake). Yet she is burning, burning.

Let us put it out. No firestorm of blame would be raging in Victorian papers or in Canberra nor would Christine Nixon herself be scorched by it, were she not a woman, a decent woman, a strong woman, a prominent woman and an ethically sound woman of an age and with the experience to possess a raging integrity of her own and, by her very being, to offer ruthless men a soft target.

Julia Baird wrote in *Media Tarts*, her book about press treatment of women politicians:

… when they show emotion, make mistakes or behave like the men in playing political hardball, they are fiercely castigated … if they crack under the pressure, the ensuring criticism makes it clear we actually want them to be superhuman.'

Anyone who, as Christine Nixon did, takes the lead in the war zone of policing is in exactly the same position.

Let us admit our own mistakes. One would be to blame 'the media' for it all, and I don't. Our attitudes to strong women are grievously at fault. The other would be to fail to acknowledge that even saints are fully, humanly fallible. Christine Nixon's flaw is a noble one: the learned law of all women, to accept personal responsibility.

The visibility and scrutiny of women leaders has taken changing forms over the past two or three decades, with social and other less regulated media outlets gaining traction in photographic representation and coverage of news. When Victoria's first female premier, the late Joan Kirner, was routinely drawn in cartoons in a spotted dress, it was intended to reduce her to being 'just a harassed housewife' without any serious credentials for leadership. In her co-authored book with Moira Rayner, *The Women's Power Handbook*, Kirner says she was initially hurt and distressed by these cartoons. Then she confronted the cartoonists and realised that she was playing into their hands and stopped taking it personally. She made a point then of appearing in the media in positions of control, as well as showing her humour by featuring in a fundraiser, 'Spot on Joan' and later dressed in motorbike leathers as a heavy metal guitarist. The cartoons of yesteryear look positively benign alongside many contemporary portrayals of women leaders.

Cartoons have a history of allowing for unfiltered prejudices, but social media has swept away remaining barriers to sexist and racist commentary, as Australian commentator and feminist Anne Summers has noted.[5] Reflecting on Summers' 1975 argument in *Damned Whores and God's Police,* that there are only two roles available to women—good woman and bad woman—former Australian Prime Minister Julia Gillard said, 'I was never going to be portrayed as a good woman. So, I must be the bad woman, a scheming shrew, a heartless harridan or a lying bitch.'[6] While she was Prime Minister, Gillard was subjected to an orchestrated media campaign designed to ridicule her as a woman and undermine her qualifications for leadership.[7] Gillard endured degrading, sexualised cartoons and commentary, some under the auspices of Liberal Party dinner fundraisers and at political rallies. These images reproduced in the daily media undoubtedly contributed to a loss of confidence in some quarters in her leadership.[8]

Visual images play a key role in the construction of leadership.[9] How the media chooses photographs, especially of women, can consolidate or undermine leadership reputations, convey trustworthiness or plant doubt. In another example, when Christine was a respondent in a court case in May 2016, several very different photographs of her appeared. Christine was, of course, aware that the media would be at the court case, and there were many pictures taken throughout the trial, but the editors were after the 'money shot', which they thought they got. In its choices of photographs, the media told its readers what to think, portraying Christine looking stressed and sick at the start of the case, so much so that friends contacted her to ask if she was all right. As the case unfolded with a lack of sensationalism and evidence, it became obvious to all, including the media, that there was no case to answer. The media subsided and the photos selected by them portrayed Christine looking strong and confident just a couple of days later. Two months later the judge found in favour of Christine and two other senior police.

The phenomenon of women's leadership being judged on the basis of appearance and bodies is also seen internationally. British research has documented a stream of commentary on women politicians: their cleavage, clothing and shoes, segmenting them into 'motherly nags, menopausal harpies and phwoar-inducing stunners'.[10] Bodies and clothing are treated as 'fair game', a basis for drawing conclusions about women's character and 'fitness' for leadership. When media coverage directs attention to bodies, it drives out recognition of the person's achievements or track record. In the 2016 US election, opponents of Hillary Clinton and other female candidates charged that they didn't have 'the look of leadership'. The 2011 US film *Miss Representation* identified many other international examples of women leaders being disparaged, and showed the impact on young women, who are deterred from aspiring to leadership. These dynamics are encountered in the ostensibly professional domains of law firms and hallowed executive suites as much as building sites, and by junior and senior women alike.[11]

Why and how do bodies matter in leadership?

It is important to remember that leadership is not something an individual has, but something that is bestowed by others. While anyone can occupy a position of authority, leadership needs to be recognised by supporters, colleagues or followers. Research shows that societies and communities are often captive to gender stereotypes in this process.[12] That is, they are more likely to attribute leadership—at least initially—to those who 'look' like a leader according to historical and cultural conventions. Tall, attractive men have more frequently been favoured for and elevated to leadership, even when they have few of the skills or capabilities required. Popular commentator Malcolm Gladwell has termed this 'The Warren Harding Effect', after the infamous, ineffective American president who was elected purely on the basis that he was tall and handsome and had the 'look' of a president.

Amanda's research looking at images of leaders in the media over a long period of time finds that white, male leaders' bodies usually enjoy the privilege of not being 'seen'.[13] The media is complicit in making men look more leader-like. Men are pictured fully suited, often with their hands concealed in their pockets, with the only skin revealed being the face. Often they are photographed as a 'headshot'. If their body is included it is usually in front of a pillar or other architectural monument that symbolises strength, and more likely to be portrayed in ways that reinforce masculinity and invincibility. Often there is a mythology of physical strength that is cultivated, as in the case of Russian President Vladimir Putin. In a less caricatured example, American President Franklin D Roosevelt, who was paralysed for most of his political life, was almost always officially photographed propped up by a colleague or swimming, but rarely in his wheelchair.

Women, including women leaders, are often appraised as womanly bodies first, not just as themselves but representing all women, including sexualities, pregnancy and mothering. Reducing women to their bodies and gendered stereotypes is a time-honoured way for people to cope with anxieties about women with power. Historians of women's leadership have shown how women have been constructed as unsuitable for leadership. They are cast as too weak and fragile, too foolish and hysterical, too passionate, subject to bodily desires and therefore immoral, too captive to their roles as child bearers, and so on. Women's bodies have made them 'unfit' for leadership.[14]

The combined effects of these portrayals make most women's paths in leadership more difficult. They encounter expectations that they will represent all women and embody the feminine stereotype that women should only seek opportunities for the collective good, not for their own advancement.[15] As portrayed in Figure 10.1, women are subject to multiple contradictory pressures: to be successful they must be concerned about how they look (cultivating a not-too-ambitious or power-hungry demeanour), but they should not *look* like they are worried about how they look, because they then appear self-absorbed, rather than being suitably concerned about the common good.

Responding to visibility and bodily stereotypes

A common accompaniment to this physical scrutiny is to advise women to 'tailor' themselves to male norms. An extensive literature advises them on image management, and colour and wardrobe consultants—many corporate sponsored—teach women to dress to a formula. For example, in 2015 Melbourne City Council hired an image consultant to teach its senior—mainly women—officers 'The Art of Authentic Self-Packaging: What dressing for success really means'. Although the program was cancelled when women councillors found out about it, it is common for women to be counselled on their dress and appearance in ways that men aren't. Encouraged to camouflage their gender, women are told to wear pared-back

Figure 10.1: Multiple pressures on women leaders

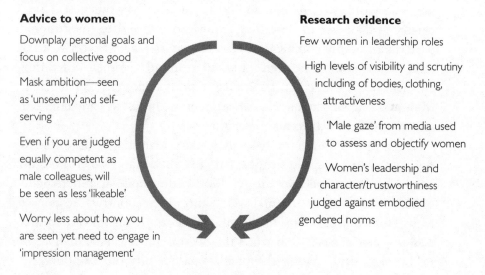

Advice to women

Downplay personal goals and focus on collective good

Mask ambition—seen as 'unseemly' and self-serving

Even if you are judged equally competent as male colleagues, will be seen as less 'likeable'

Worry less about how you are seen yet need to engage in 'impression management'

Research evidence

Few women in leadership roles

High levels of visibility and scrutiny including of bodies, clothing, attractiveness

'Male gaze' from media used to assess and objectify women

Women's leadership and character/trustworthiness judged against embodied gendered norms business suits that don't show too much leg while also avoiding trousers that are 'butch' and flats or heels that are too high. At a more profound level, research documents the extremes some women feel they need to go to, such as self-medication to manage menstruation and menopause and surgically timing childbirth to minimise the effects on their employer and career.

In our own work with women leaders, we explore the dynamics of visibility and scrutiny by helping women understand that these processes are not about them, but about how society and organisations often respond to the discomfort of difference and women with power. As a first principle, those of us involved and interested in leadership should recognise that what we are describing here is beyond women's control. Because visibility and 'standing out' are not situations that women can have influence over, no amount of careful dressing or self-presentation will reduce scrutiny or prevent comments. Our first commitment must be to contribute to wider organisational and societal efforts to change the embodied norms by which women are judged. At the very least, this can often be valuable for women to recognise. It helps to know that a comment about our clothes says more about the discomfort of the speaker and their obsolete norms than providing any imperative to change!

While it is important to expose the double standards by which men and women are judged bodily and physically, women also have agency and power in how they choose to respond to institutional patterns of bodily commentary—as is seen in Tracey Spicer's TEDx talk. There is no 'one right way' to respond. Women are different from each other and they have various experiences. Particular responses will suit women in various sectors, industries and contexts and over different life and career stages.

Amanda's research of women leaders identifies four different positions regarding physicality and sexuality that women take up over time and when they are working within male-dominated cultures.[16] The four quadrants (see Figure 10.2) contrast responses from women when they have little versus more significant formal power (vertical axis), and when they adopt a low versus high sense of their identity as women or their sexual identity (horizontal axis).

A low sense of sexual identity means they think of themselves as professionals or managers whose gender and sexuality are irrelevant to how they do their job. In contrast a high sense of sexual identity means women consciously acknowledge that aspects of them as women—their values, approach to leadership, style of influencing and so on—underpin how they go about their work as leaders.

When women are relatively new entrants to their professions and organisations and have low positional power, they typically expect that they will be treated on the basis of merit, and this is as it should be (Quadrant 1). Typically, women in this quadrant are surprised when they are singled out for special attention and are uninterested in efforts to support other women. They want to be treated on and rewarded for their merit. However, and particularly in traditionally male-dominated environments, women can then begin to experience increased attention and visibility *as women*. For example, they encounter remarks about their body, attractiveness or availability, their perceived level of ambition or eligibility to belong (Quadrant 2). There may be speculation about their relationship status or their likelihood of starting a family (and therefore taking

Figure 10.2: Contrasting responses of women to visibility as women

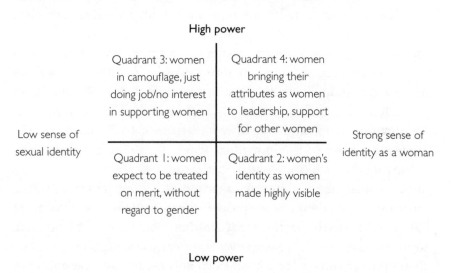

maternity leave), which in turn influences mobility and career decisions made by superiors.

These assessments on the basis of sex not capability come as a shock to most women. Despite their surprise, our work with many women indicates these processes of highlighting women's gender and sexuality are still widespread across sectors, as likely to occur in professional services as in engineering. Women often respond by choosing their clothing to minimise attention and comment—innocuous pantsuits, blouses with high necks, loose-fitting tops and shoes with flat or low heels.

What about senior women advising more junior women on dress? One seasoned bureaucrat who has spent her career guiding teachers advises the young women she mentors: 'If you can see through it, up it or down it, don't wear it!' Research indicates that such advice is often unwelcome and can be seen as 'policing' a masculine-defined order, being patronising, or even being insulting to other women. The value of such advice to the person receiving it will depend on the relationship, level of trust and how they perceive the intention of the advice giver.

Although there are some circumstances when it's good to ignore comments about specific bodies, ignoring is one of the ways that discriminatory gendered cultures get perpetuated. As senior women, we believe it is always good to speak up about inappropriate comments about yourself or other women in a way that draws attention away from the individual woman towards the broader phenomenon and its effects. A likely response from some male colleagues is to accuse you of not having a sense of humour or being oversensitive. Ignore this reaction and keep drawing attention to the damage sexist comments cause to the individual woman's confidence and to the culture where such comments become routine.

As women acquire more power and credibility in their careers, circumstances change and propel them to make a choice. In Quadrant 3 are those who maintain that women should be treated on merit and that they themselves have earned leadership based on their own capability. These women usually eschew any mentoring or advocacy of other women in their profession or organisation, and they may seek to minimise their own visibility as women. Many are ideologically opposed to the use of quotas or targets, arguing that they can often rebound on women who struggle to be seen as having been appointed on merit.

Increasingly, though, we see many senior women leaders—in business, the public sector and conservative areas of politics—in Quadrant 4. The idea that good women will naturally bubble up into leadership positions has now been countered by decades of research and evidence, as we discussed in chapter 2. Quadrant 4 contains those women who have earned leadership roles but also explicitly bring their qualities and concerns as women to the way they lead. They are also likely to use their power and influence to name discriminatory norms, make workplaces more inclusive and help support other women into leadership roles.

An example of owning one's identity as a woman in leadership comes from Christine's speech at her inauguration as Victorian Chief Police Commissioner, which we discussed earlier. Although she was advised to keep her swearing-in a low-key occasion, for a variety of reasons she decided to opt for a more public event.[17] In her speech, which was widely quoted in the media, Christine identified herself as a woman and that her values and experiences as a woman would shape how she led Victoria Police. This act of self-identification as a woman is highly unusual in leadership but for Christine it was a very important way of signalling that she was interested in change and would do the job of leading police in ways that reflected her own identifications as a woman: to community and her values of justice and equity.

Another example of Quadrant 4 leadership is Julia Gillard's famous misogyny speech when she was Prime Minister. In that speech, which went 'viral' internationally and is probably one of the things Gillard is most recognised for, she named the sexism to which she and other Australian women were subject. In her view 'calling the sexism out is not playing the victim … It is the only strategy that will enable change.'[18]

When we present the framework in Figure 10.2, it is sometimes assumed that women in Quadrant 4 have to conform to an ideal of 'womanliness', femininity or feminism. Rather, what we are interested in is leadership by women that is *not about* conforming to a dominant template but invites expression of what is important to them as women. Amanda's research with her colleague Professor Emma Bell has looked at film and television examples as sources of new insight about how women leaders respond to these processes in ways that affirm the values, approaches, bodies and intent that women may bring to leadership.[19] In a detailed case study looking at the Danish TV series *Borgen*, Emma and Amanda explore representations of women leaders as influential, embodied protagonists. The three series of *Borgen* portray a woman politician in a minor party who becomes Prime Minister of Denmark. Over the course of the three series, Birgitte is initially triumphant, then challenged by family demands to step back from politics. She becomes an international board member and speaker for a time, before starting a new political party. Her career story is interwoven with her personal story, including her separation then divorce from her husband, her daughter's battle with mental illness and her own with cancer. There are also other key women characters in leadership, including Katrine, a TV anchor and journalist, Hanne, another journalist, and Pia, a producer.

Through Emma and Amanda's analysis of the show they identify three categories of response that women can adopt in leadership within cultures that have been created and shaped by men around the men's own interests. These are:

1. disrupting the patriarchal order

2. exploring an alternative 'feminine imaginary'

3. erotic leadership.

Disrupting the patriarchal order includes those situations of naming and rejecting the norms by which women are judged differently in leadership. In *Borgen,* an example is where Birgitte as the new Prime Minister comes under a lot of pressure to look the part on election night. She shares this in her first televised address, saying that people can expect something more genuine and values-based from her and her party than a groomed image or a pre-worked speech.

The idea of cultivating an alternative feminine imaginary comes from the work of feminists and philosophers—for example, Belgian Luce Irigaray, who advocates honouring the connection women potentially have to their bodies, their senses and nature as guides for living and, we suggest, leadership.[20] An example from *Borgen* is Birgitte's decision and negotiation to take leave from being Prime Minister to care for her depressed daughter. Inevitably this is seen by the media and others in government, including her own party, as evidence of not being 'fit' to lead, and that she should resign. Yet Birgitte resists such pressures, maintaining that she can be both leader and carer—she doesn't have to choose—and she then returns to her role refocused.

Exercising 'erotic leadership' is another option that involves recognising and involving the body, pleasure and physicality in the influencing and change work of leadership.[21] While the erotic in organisational life has come to be narrowly defined as sexual, its fuller meaning emphasises the importance of putting a value on pleasure and love in how we interact with others. How can eros and pleasure be part of leadership? Organisational communications academics Suzy D'Enbeau and Patrice Buzzanell explore 'erotic heroines' in popular culture forms such as the TV show *Mad Men*. Their analysis reveals women valuing eros and pleasure in activities such as leadership and mentoring, rather than being forced to repress their sense of themselves as women. Popular culture, Emma and Amanda have suggested, may provide forums for women to imagine, create and see leadership being done differently, as an embrace of bodies, care and eros rather than the traditional requirement for women to suppress these parts of themselves to survive in organisations.[22]

Women leaders come under pressure from the media, peers and bosses, men and other women to camouflage and manage their femaleness, bodies and physicality to conform to a narrow set of ideals. We regard such conformity as not sustainable for individual women or in the collective interests of women, many of whom do not conform to such ideals but have much to offer. Further, there is increasing evidence from cognitive science that our bodies shape our minds, our sense of confidence and efficacy, which in turn is registered by those around us. For example, Harvard researcher Amy Cuddy advises to 'let your body tell you that you're powerful and deserving and you'll become more present, enthusiastic and authentically yourself'. The text that follows draws together research and experience on how women can challenge criticism of, and be comfortable in, their physical selves.

What women leaders can do in response to visibility and scrutiny

1. Resist excessive grooming pressures and organisational norms that prescribe how women should dress and look.

2. Don't assume that acceptance or success requires conformity to dominant norms—trying to look like a man or blend in doesn't guarantee success or necessarily bring credibility.

3. Understand that comments about your appearance say nothing about your leadership, only about the commentator.

4. Notice and name when other women are victims of derogatory and sexist comments.

5. Don't be part of organisational efforts to monitor women's appearance and don't ignore cultures that normalise commentary on women's bodies or attractiveness—if you find yourself about to judge another woman's appearance, stop and think again about the impacts on you, her and society.

6. Speak out against the double standards by which women and men are judged physically.

7. Call out and disrupt norms of physical camouflage or grooming that work against women.

8. Be aware that women will come under different pressures around physicality depending on their experience and power—don't assume others will share your experience or benefit from your path.

9. When mentoring, coaching and advising, trust and support women's confidence and decision-making in matters of physicality. Don't assume you know best.

10. Be open to bringing your whole physical and authentic self to leadership and remember that in doing so you are paving diverse paths for others around and following you.

11. Help others understand how to deal with responses that do not welcome authenticity in women.

12. Celebrate the look of women leaders, for example, Hillary Clinton's pantsuit campaign.[23]

11
Understanding identities, stages and transitions

> *I had to find out for myself that life is not a performance sport; that achievement is a state of grace, not the sum total of relentless activity; that ego might not be a dirty word, but it can be a ruthless taskmaster; and that hard work often brings just rewards, but it's not what sets you free.*
>
> Clare Wright

The kinds of challenges we face as a leader or as a leader of change, and our approaches to them, evolve and adapt throughout our career and life. Research models and experience suggest that understanding these phases—where we are now, how others have responded in the past to comparable circumstances, and identifying the forces that hold us to certain ways of operating—provide powerful prompts for growth and learning. Pausing to explore transition points and catalysts for change help us to learn from the past, cultivate ongoing reflectiveness and get perspective during crises or major setbacks.

The ideas in this chapter are based on research into change and identity. It needs to be noted that there is a sharp distinction between change and transition. While changes include the inevitable external occurrences and disruptions in careers and lives, transition can be understood as the internal psychological processes that need to accompany change and that determine our sense of efficacy and fulfilment. Transitions can be supported by listening to others go through similar events, being open to advice and hints, as Christine describes in the next chapter when she moved on from the police force. Transitions can be supported by listening to yourself and not suppressing feelings of unhappiness or that you need to try something different, as Amanda describes in chapter 13, when she took a year off and completed her yoga teacher training.

The second core concept we draw on here is identity. Research suggests that none of us is one fixed and enduring self for the whole of our life. The identities we take on shift in response to broad context, circumstance and our own learning.[1] Although there might be some consistent values that underpin our decisions and choices over the course of our life, our roles and personal circumstances call forth a dynamic sense of self. At any one time, the self we inhabit may contain competing elements; for example, being a focused and tough decision-maker in one part of your life and a compassionate enabler in another.

It is a positive thing that we are active shapers of how we respond to circumstances. Women can and should be confident about taking on roles or activities when new and different things are demanded of us, even if we don't necessarily feel knowledgeable. Opportunities to reflect on our leadership journey and exercises such as identifying the narrative of our life or focusing on our moral compass or 'true north'[2] are valuable means for helping us identify where we are at as leaders and what is holding back a transition or potential movement to a more courageous or bold self. At the same time, we need to recognise that women leaders are subject to particular social pressures, socialised ideas of the limits on their own aspirations and gendered expectations at different stages. While most of the literature and research doesn't pay particular attention to the stages and transitions that make up women's experiences in leadership, we think they are important and worth discussing in detail.

Exploring identity as a leader
A central part of most of the leadership programs Amanda has facilitated has had a focus on identity. She was exposed to theories of

identity and childhood influences on leadership in her undergraduate degrees in politics and psychology, and pursued this interest in her doctoral and subsequent research. Supervised by two political psychologists who were psychoanalytically inclined, Amanda was always encouraged to look deeper into both herself and her research subjects and ask questions like, 'Where are these behaviours being driven from?' and 'What kinds of narratives or scripts has this person internalised about how they handle conflict or how they should be as a leader?'[3]

Amanda's experience is that helping people to reflect on their backgrounds and crucial life events provides insight—for example, into how they continue to repeat patterns of behaviour established early in life, long after those patterns have ceased to be effective or helpful.[4] The exercises generally include an exploration of:

- family background, schooling and early years and what the person felt they learned about 'how they should be' and 'how they should be as a leader'

- scripts or templates that they have been exposed to from professional training, organisational cultures, and gender and cultural backgrounds, such as 'women should be selfless and nurturing' or 'medical leaders should never show emotion'

- crises and crucibles or intense transformative experiences where the person was forced to think of themselves differently, such as moving to a new place, being an outsider, a family breakdown or significant failure

- the identity question or issue they are currently exploring, such as how to bring more of themselves to their work or how to make a big change in career.

One woman who had been very successful at a senior level attended a program we taught because she wanted help to take a new direction, and this was provided through the identity work session we ran. In that session, she realised that she had, throughout her career, always been the vital second-in-charge to a confident male leader. It was a pattern set with her older brother, who her parents held up as a model. It meant she downplayed her own intelligence and aspirations in order to make her boss look good. The program and her work with colleagues during it helped her resolve to stop repeating the pattern, and gave her the confidence to step away from the script that she had been given by her family and then internalised.

Other common scripts that women have been given in their early years include 'being the responsible one', being very conscientious and being told they've only achieved through hard work not ability, or being a 'rescuer'—that is, spending most of their time and energy making things okay for others when those others could and should have been learning to do this for themselves. Many people already recognise these patterns in themselves; for example, how they react under pressure, what they seek out when feeling needy, whether they wait for authorisation to act from someone more senior, and where some of these behaviours come from. As described in chapter 6, and following Hugh Mackay's work about human desires, most people can identify the ones that drive them most strongly. However, there are several reasons why enabling women to explore identity questions together is valuable in leadership:

- While people know things about themselves, understanding how your history and socialisation play out in shared contexts of leadership provides new insights.

- Leadership often activates 'hot buttons', such as feeling like an impostor (see chapter 9); as careers and contexts change, different aspects of identity will be brought to the fore.

- Undertaking this exploration in a safe space with other women often allows a level of vulnerability that evokes new insight into patterns—there is a difference between intellectually understanding a pattern you have and emotionally re-experiencing that pattern and its impacts, then seeing that you do not have to continue to re-enact it.[5]

- Research supports that effective leaders seek regular opportunities to reflect on where they are at, to recognise obstacles (sometimes internally perpetuated) and how to authorise themselves to be authentic and true to their values.

Coping with change and enabling transitions in leadership

Robert Kegan and Lisa Lahey are adult education researchers who bring their interest in evolving mental complexity to help leaders not just to cope, but to develop their own adaptiveness and perspective taking. In their books *How the Way We Talk Changes the Way We Work* and *Immunity to Change*, they draw on various psychological and educational models of cognitive and moral development.[6] They also reflect on changing understandings in cognitive neuroscience that show that we are able to keep on becoming more sophisticated in our capacity to handle information, step back from conflicting imperatives and foster good decision-making (see also our discussion on mindfulness in chapter 13). Kegan and Lahey identify three 'meaning systems', in ascending order of mental complexity, and we elaborate here on how leaders might experience and recognise these stages:

1. The 'socialised mind': the primary driver for the leader is what they believe others will want to hear—they go along with things to get along. They have a strong commitment to being a team player and are highly sensitive to cues about how they need to look, speak and act to be recognised as a leader. Their identity is likely to align with the beliefs and values of those important to them.

2. The 'self-authorising mind': Leaders are prepared to set their own agenda. They value independence of mind and establish their own boundaries. It is at this stage that the leader learns to lead, understanding that their value is in their ability to take advice but not be bound by group opinion.

3. The 'self-transforming mind': Only rarely is this found in senior executives; it includes the capacity to step back from and see the limits of one's own thinking. At this stage the leader recognises any one system or world view is inevitably incomplete. They are more comfortable with contradictions and holding multiple systems or world views in play. Identity is bound to this openness to self-transformation, rather than through consistency with previous beliefs.

Progress through these stages does not inevitably unfold in any leader's development, as Kegan and Lahey point out. More likely, they will be prompted by catalysts and difficult challenges, often following times of discontent, disappointment or disequilibrium. This framework, in our experience, helps leaders validate different forms of leadership that involve not just standing back and gaining perspective, but the extra step we described earlier of 'getting on the balcony of oneself'—that is, of observing and reflecting on your own ideologies and beliefs in play. Although this may sound like a lengthy or unduly self-absorbed process, the psychological and neurological evidence is that, on the contrary, it is almost always beneficial for ourselves and others requiring less, not more, rumination.[7]

According to the work of psychological researchers such as Gail Sheehy[8] and organisational change researchers such as William Bridges, new stages are often preceded by disequilibrium and uncertainty. To be open to undergoing the internal psychological process of transition—as distinct from the external process of change—involves taking ownership of what has gone before, the way your habits and ways of acting may have contributed to an increasingly unsatisfactory status quo. It can involve a deadened period where usually purposeful activities lose meaning. You then often enter what Sheehy terms a 'passage' during which you have the potential to make healthy adaptation or alternatively to get marooned in change-avoiding or defensive behaviours.

Women leaders often experience hurdles and setbacks at various transition points that are a product of discriminatory stereotypes and norms. Those working in conservative or traditionally male-dominated environments are singled out because of their gender as 'not one of us', and hence they are likely to be catapulted into Kegan and Lahey's second stage as they grapple with what they are working for and what difference they want to make. They begin to recognise that leadership may require taking a dissenting view and speaking out rather than toeing a line or even just doing the job.

The changing ways others see women as they mature was the subject of doctoral research by one of Amanda's students, Alyson Meister.[9] Younger women and those in child-bearing stages often experience a high degree of visibility early in their careers as their physicality, sexuality, availability and likelihood of having children are all speculated upon by colleagues and bosses. While it is illegal to ask women directly about their plans to become pregnant, young women say this is a constant informal subject of speculation in selection and promotion decisions. Older and more senior women experience different kinds of challenges to their leadership. They may be informally categorised as 'too difficult' because they are often less willing to censor their views or deliver excessive working hours. They may be dismissed as 'not tough enough' or 'not committed enough' to assume demanding leadership roles.

There is value in helping women be prepared for some of these not uncommon experiences as they progress and become more senior. On the positive side, Sheehy's research for *New Passages* also suggests that women are often beneficiaries of the opportunity of a 'second adulthood'—that is, the period after around forty-five, when they may, for a variety of reasons, feel freer and more confident to make profound changes in how they work as well as how they live. Sheehy shows that broader improvements in many social, economic and health systems offer a potential period of health, optimism, choice and connection long after previous generations would have expected to survive, and that this opportunity is particularly taken up by women.

Women change too, some becoming more comfortable in being themselves or to reveal in their leadership more of what they consider to be their authentic selves—their histories and values, triumphs and failures. Leadership and gender researchers Herminia Ibarra, Robin Ely and Deborah Kolb argue that all people become leaders via an iterative identity shift.[10] The process of being offered and tested by opportunities and challenges is likely to be much more littered with submerged stereotypes and subtle discriminatory norms for women leaders than their male counterparts. They show how these experiences are usually unexpected among women aspiring to leadership. Women leaders can feel ambushed by them, and this is another reason to have an eyes-wide-open understanding of obstacles in moving through career stages. Women also vary in their willingness to identify themselves as advocates for other women or to self-identify as feminists.[11]

How and why do women come to support other women?

One of the most rewarding aspects of running women-in-leadership programs is to experience diverse groups of women opening up to, trusting and learning from each other. The groups we teach usually include women just about to take big steps up in their career, others keen to step sideways into new areas, or those ready to step off. Many are keen to restore hope and positivity after tough experiences. Groups also contain those who are articulate and confident feminists, with others ambivalent or dismissive of this label. Among young women, particularly, self-identifying as a feminist may have attracted derision or condemnation in workplaces. Some feel an affinity with other women. Many do not, and are quick to volunteer that senior women have not been supporters of them in their career.

Memoirs by women leaders, such as American stateswoman Madeleine Albright's *Madam Secretary*, Hillary Clinton's *Hard Choices* and Facebook COO Sheryl Sandberg's description of her journey in *Lean In*, describe varied, often belated preparedness to self-identify as women and support other women. Women leaders chronicle a stop-and-start process, whereby off-the-shelf feminist convictions and ideologies get moulded and reworked by personal circumstance. Understanding the pressures and phases women encounter in the process of speaking up for other women helps promote self-compassion and courage, as well as offering practical strategies for surviving and leading well.

In her own journey coming to recognise the obstacles to women in leadership, Amanda experienced several stages of growing awareness of the issues and determination to do something about them.[12] Each was propelled by particular catalysts:

- listening to and learning from other women, including deepening admiration for what other women have endured and changed in order for the women that follow to thrive

- needing to better explain her own experience—initially in a world of work dominated by men and later through her observations about how the world of leadership was set up for particular men

- encountering resistance, feeling disillusioned but also realising the need for men—not just women—to take ownership of change

- discovering that we can all have impact but we need to work with allies and partners, not alone; that we need to not get captured by polite or incremental solutions that don't change things; and that we need to share and talk about what's really happening.

Amanda's experience of these catalysts

A recent MBA student of mine was lamenting that while the need for feminism was clear to her, among her friends it was more common to view feminism as:

- not necessary—we've achieved equality

- outdated—an old solution to a superseded problem

- extreme—the domain of man-haters and lesbians.

It prompted me to reflect on my own journey of belated awareness of the issues facing women in society and in leadership.

Listening to and learning from other women
In the early 1980s I was struggling through the last stages of my PhD. My husband had just left me and I was pregnant with our daughter. My son was two. I had little time but needed money. An opportunity to be a researcher for a project exploring women in Victorian local government—or more accurately the lack of them—came up. Since their inception, over a century earlier, local councils had been the exclusively male domains of property developers, landowners and engineers who often benefited in material ways from being on council.

My first encounter with 'real' feminists was through this project: an impressive group that formed the steering committee for my research.[13] All of them had been successfully elected to local government councils through the late 1970s and early 1980s as part of a mixed surge of community, urban and environmental activism alongside second-wave feminism. In rural areas women were elected from more traditional platforms of wanting a different community voice. Often they were the first women on council and most of them endured sexism and sabotage—from polite putdowns to hair-raising misogyny—on the way to being elected and then once on council. Many were members of women's groups, both progressive ones such as EMILY's List and the Women's Electoral Lobby (WEL), which campaigned for more women to be elected to all levels of Australian government, and traditional bodies such as the Australian Local Government Women's Association and the Country Women's Association.

I had completed my undergraduate study in the mid 1970s. It was a time of upheaval and questioning, of exciting rejuvenation of second-wave feminism through the work of people like Germaine Greer, Bella Abzug, Betty Friedan and Gloria Steinem. More controversial were the radical feminist movements that were interested in women's sexuality, such as described by Shere Hite in her *Hite Report*, vaginal versus clitoral orgasms, advocates for more than penetrative sex, and so on. Yet I was sheltered. Equipped with a convenient cynicism about activism, which was really just a cloak for complacency—I hesitate, appalled, as I write this—I wondered what all the feminist fuss was about.

What helped me get real and in touch with feminism was the research of women councillors—women in remote rural towns and gritty inner-urban suburbs—who spoke graphically about their lives, their experiences of being belittled and subordinated and having the issues they cared about—for example, protecting communities from freeways and harsh developments that would evict long-term residents—trivialised as women's concerns. I wrote a journal article and some newspaper columns suggesting that women in leadership were a phenomenon we should be supporting. The journal rejected my article as 'not serious' political science.

This research also showed me women joining together to change things. I'd grown up with brothers and no sisters and, despite having close female friends, I hadn't seen women working together and running things. This research showed me that while women alone had limited impact, women together—even with diverse backgrounds—could look to influence big social reforms.

Needing to better explain my own experience

On graduating I got a job as a social planner with a federal government body. I enjoyed that job, and the subsequent one in consulting, and learned a lot in the multidisciplinary teams that I was working in—usually as the lone woman. The (universally male) engineers and economists won the day. All the other women in the organisation were secretaries or receptionists or condemned to the typing pool—a room where women sat at desks in rows all day typing the reports and weighty correspondence of the men. Each of these organisational experiences provided powerful insights into the degree and impacts of sex-segregated work environments. While I puzzled about why my views were ignored, I still didn't think it had much to do with gender.

It wasn't until I began lecturing at the Melbourne Business School in 1988 that I started to see the bigger shape and impacts of the systematic exclusion of women in organisations and from opportunities for leadership. It wasn't just an absence. There were policies, norms and processes in business and in management education that meant, for example, that only a very few women were able to apply for and undertake an MBA. In the early days (1980s and early 1990s) employers sponsored most MBA students by giving them time off or, in some cases, continuing to provide them with a salary while the students studied. Few women could obtain an employer's sponsorship. Also, they were invariably earning less than their male counterparts.

Another barrier was that most MBA programs were inflexible and had to be completed within a limited time. There was no leave provision for women who needed to take a break or reduce their commitment due to child bearing or family responsibilities. These obstacles were glaringly obvious to me because I was in the boat of having to juggle work and lecturing with a young family. Yet these barriers weren't seen by the mostly male 'fish' swimming in (and benefiting from) the dominant system. When I tried to draw attention to these discriminatory barriers, the most common response was, 'Oh, Amanda, are you sure you're not imagining these things?'

Initially I wondered whether I was and then castigated myself for being difficult and whingey. Increasingly, though, with the benefit of research and sharing stories with women colleagues, I realised that this, too, was part of the way cultures denied women's experiences and shut down opportunities and possibilities for change. Speaking up, we are often made to feel like troublemakers. We become unpopular and unlikeable.[14]

I became—belatedly and feeling ill-equipped—a feminist. I couldn't understand what I was seeing and experiencing until I started to read and research gender and theories of how and why societies and organisations subordinate women. It was also an enormously freeing step to do this as it helped explain my own experience of being rejected, put down and marginalised. It helped me understand that the routine and insidious ways this subordination occurred weren't due to me or my failure to navigate my career better. It was the way that most traditional, male-dominated organisations worked, retaining power and privilege in the hands of elites (academic, political, bureaucratic) and ensuring the status quo remained and served their interests.

Encountering resistance, feeling disillusioned

By the 1990s I started to write about how gender played out in organisations and leadership, and in my own experiences as an academic in a business-school setting. I was advised by one of the most senior academics not to do gender research, and in a later interview for a University Chair I was encouraged to stress my interest in 'diversity' rather than gender. An interest only in gender branded me as narrow and 'less promotable'.

Doing gender work was, and remains, difficult and unpopular. There are many structural and internal pressures to not be seen or identified as advocating for opportunities for women. In my teaching, many male and female students assume I will be pushing a feminist barrow. Invited to speak on gender issues, most business audiences expect that I will politely talk about strategies that 'help' women, like mentoring or family leave provisions. When I describe templates of heroic masculinity in leadership as the problem holding things back—rather than women—audiences grow very still and judgements and fear fill the air.

I realised, too, that when I positioned myself as an advocate for reform I let lots of others off the hook. In my activity, I gave the impression that there was more improvement happening than there actually was. This dynamic occurred for other women leaders—the more they took up the role of advocating for women, the more their male peers sat back and said, 'Well, thank goodness that's taken care of.'

Discovering we can all have impact

A substantial part of my research and teaching in leadership has arisen from my recognition that it's not women that must change to step up for leadership roles but our very constructs and assumptions about leadership. Narrow templates that demand total commitment to a heroic regime serve no one—the leader, their followers, society or its needs for innovation, adaption, sustainability. Changing such templates is a big undertaking but a worthwhile one, and I come across lots of women and men doing just that by doing leadership differently.

Yet the evidence is that many corporate approaches to improving gender equality haven't had much impact on opportunities for women in senior leadership. As we describe in chapter 3, the gender pay gap is still large and the number of women in top-level jobs remains proportionately tiny. In my view, this is primarily because these approaches are incremental not innovative; they help women get a leg up or fairer treatment rather than changing underlying leadership cultures. We act as if the exclusion of women will be remedied by rational 'human capital' arguments, rather than addressing power and the attractions of working in homogeneous groups.

Speaking out about such issues, revealing the problems with relying on economic incentives or human capital logic, and why quotas, for example, may need to be considered, requires persistence and personal courage.[15] It requires us to name practices and norms that we know exist but are seen as just the way things are done.

Both Christine and I have got less worried about speaking out. We don't underestimate the value of formal power and authority, which have provided platforms for us both to work for change, but having a firm grasp on the research and evidence gives us understanding and resolve. The ideas of mindfulness and 'less ego' leadership discussed in the following chapters have helped restore resilience when encountering all the ways resistance to women's equality gets re-manifested in continuing sexist workplace cultures and harassment, social media attacks on women, family violence and so on.

So, too, has working alongside inspiring women who in different spheres, support and inspire their colleagues and make leadership more open to women.

12

Managing and reducing risks

> *Fear can be healthy. Fear of stuffing up provides a potent incentive to keep us honest, ensure we do our homework, apply ourselves fully, no short cuts.*
>
> Christine Nixon, 2011

Leadership is risky. Most leaders, and especially perhaps women leaders, have times when they feel both professional and personal risks very directly. When we ask groups of women about the risks they experience, they identify the following:

Professional

- being locked out of the action

- reputational damage

- martyrdom

- 'assassination'

- being typecast

Personal

- family—taking time off, turning down assignments or not doing so and coping with resentment or alienation from family

- losing connections with friends and family

- fear and anxiety, manifesting as illness and stress

- feeling like an impostor

- partners—negotiating support but also finding ways to give it.

These risks are very real to women, who spend energy and time worrying about them. Following are research and some strategies from our own experience for handling professional and personal risks in the interests of helping leaders be resilient and flourish, beginning with a focus on the broader professional and organisational level—how to shape expectations and conduct yourself in the contexts of leadership. We then move to strategies for managing risk at the more personal level, which we also explore further in the next chapter, adding approaches to resilience and renewal in leadership.

Reflect on and know what leadership is for you

We have emphasised that there are many problems with conventional views of leaders and leadership, not least for the leader herself. Ronald Heifetz, a leadership expert from Harvard University's Kennedy School, writes on the challenge of 'staying alive' in leadership. He identifies key sources of risk as the templates or myths of leadership to which we hold ourselves.[1] In his first book—fittingly called *Leadership Without Easy Answers*—he suggests that the myth of leadership is the myth of the lone warrior, the solitary individual whose heroism and brilliance enable him to lead the way.[2]

This myth brings with it many risks for leaders. It suggests that only a small number of particular people—read 'men'—are fit to lead. It excludes others who might want to lead but don't fit the mould. It also brings with it another myth: that people are born to lead. While there is little research to support the idea that leadership can only be done by a uniquely brilliant and brave few, it is a popular narrative that can trip up both the leader—who doubts herself—and her followers. A third fallacy is that leadership is done alone using your own wit and wisdom. The risks of this myth include seducing leaders into isolating themselves, confusing individual cleverness for leadership and personal brilliance for courage. A final fallacy is that leaders think their job is to problem-solve for others, rather than help the people who need to adapt or find new ways forward to solve the problem themselves. Although occasionally leaders do need to problem-solve, far more often leadership involves providing a space or container through which those who implement change come up with new ways forward.

The remedy for these risks is to explore alternative and, we argue, women-centred understandings of leadership. Leaders need to articulate to themselves and others that the leadership they will try and enact takes a collaborative, less individualistic and ego-driven view. This kind of leadership sees the key task as supporting and mobilising others to exercise creativity and take responsibility. The next strategy we describe directly addresses this point.

Get perspective—'get on the balcony'

Effective leadership often involves both being part of the action and being able to gain perspective on it, to step back and diagnose what the whole group or system needs at a particular point in time. Described and popularised by Heifetz and his colleagues as moving between the balcony and the dance floor, the basic idea is to take a step back from the situation you are in and get some perspective.

Christine remembers trying to convey this idea to senior police in New South Wales. Instead of the balcony and the dance floor analogy, she turned to football. Jack Gibson was a famous NSW Rugby League football coach of the 1970s. He was very successful, and a man of few words. He was one of the first coaches to depart from the old idea that the captain and the coach were the same people. Instead, as a coach, he got up in the stands to watch the game instead. These days this practice—of gaining perspective and looking at the bigger picture of how a game is working—is supported by a huge array of statistics about plays, commitment, tackles and so on (some would say too much). But for the group Christine was encouraging to think differently about leadership, the metaphor was apt. It emphasises the value of taking time out, seeking alternative views and information about a situation, and developing the capacity to read group dynamics and feed them back to the group to help them reflect on how a process or problem is being understood and how they might move forward differently.

Amanda and her colleagues work with the same ideas in leadership development, encouraging participants to move between being involved—debating ideas and sharing experiences on the dance floor—and stepping back to observe and diagnose group process from the balcony. Sometimes the most powerful leadership interventions in a group's learning processes come from a balcony observation. It is also valuable to notice when you may have gone into 'the cloakroom'.[3] When things get challenging in leadership it is understandable that people want to retreat but it is important not to confuse getting on the balcony with moving in with the cloaks—where it's dark and cosy but nothing much happens.

Further, Amanda adds to the analogy by suggesting leaders get on the balcony not just to see the organisational action, but to see themselves. The preceding and next chapters provide different approaches to stepping back from yourself and your ego needs. Most of us know when we've got too caught up, overinvested in a particular outcome or process. It can be as simple as recognising when we re-enact old patterns or react to what 'presses our buttons'.[4] When leadership is coming from this ego-driven place it's usually not effective, and just recognising this is sufficient to reorient, perhaps seek independent advice or support, and proceed differently.

Encourage people to do the work

Leaders tend to take on a great deal of responsibility, but to be effective it is the broader group—the family, community, team, organisation or nation—who must collectively do the work of changing understandings or behaviours, adapting to new circumstances or creating new ways of thinking.

During all our workshops, participants do a range of activities that require them to challenge themselves, read research, listen to advice from other participants and reflect on their own thinking. We suggest to them that it's they who must do the work—we just provide the opportunities and frameworks for change. This is often unexpected. People attend seminars and courses expecting tips, and sometimes they mimic the call that many of their teams give them: 'Just tell us what to do' or 'Just tell us where we are going'. However, because most have had responsibilities for trying to implement change, they know that just giving answers won't provide sustainable innovation or change. Unless such adaptation comes from, and is owned by, the group, any change will just be tokenistic. Leaders need followers who are prepared to be part of the change. If no change occurs in the group, then the leader has not achieved one of the key tests of leadership.

In Victoria Police, when Crime Department head Assistant Commissioner Simon Overland was promoted, an opportunity was created for the seven senior managers to step up and continue to lead the change. They were offered the opportunity to form a Board of Management. The work they did led to the reform of the Crime Department, which could not have been accomplished by one or even just a few of those individuals. It required them all to take responsibility.

Find partners and allies

As we describe in the opening chapters, finding and working with partners and allies is central to our work, individually and when we work together. Christine recalls learning early the reality that none of us ever lead well if alone, that we need partners to sustain us. Even in her childhood street gang, she could rely on her friend Denise as partner and enforcer. As she wrote in *Fair Cop*:

> I am the product of many partnerships with people who have worked with me, supported and encouraged me over the years.

> Parents are partners; my brothers and friends are partners; so are the women whose solidarity and companionship buoyed me through many difficult years, and still does today ... And, of course, my husband John. Partnerships keep you real, allow you to keep focused, keep your feet on the ground. Whether you are running a household or a corporation, you need the support and belief of the people around you. Recognise and give thanks for partnerships that got you there and hold you there.

Amanda came to learn how vital partners were later. The first thing she found was that partners are often found in surprising places. When she was introducing yoga classes and non-conventional subject matter into the Business School, it was often the support staff—the facilities guys, the IT and office staff—who were behind her and let her know this. They helped make things work for her, came along to sessions or just spoke very encouraging words when the other more formal messages she was getting were that what she was doing was 'weird' and 'not appropriate' for this professional context. It's worth watching for and noticing those seemingly unlikely allies and partners.

Following these experiences, Amanda realised that she also has stereotypes about people and that many of these are misplaced. It is always good to go into new groups or difficult meetings respecting the views of others present and believing that at some level they will be open and interested. It turns out that if you set out with this mindset, allies and supporters can be found in most difficult situations.

Listen and invite others in

Listening is an important part of understanding the team, organisation or community. Listening well helps you understand what's happening in the organisation and your responses to it. How are people coping with changes? Is there too much going on already, or could people be challenged more?

As we described at the beginning, in 2001 Christine invited Amanda to come and observe her across the varied range of her roles and activities, to assist her to get some perspectives on how she was acting and what the impacts of those actions were. Amanda sat in on meetings and watched the interaction. Christine hired and invited many other outsiders in as well—an unheard-of manoeuvre at the time. They included corporate experts and academic researchers who observed and provided feedback and reviews, fresh energy, urgency or balance to a project. As an example, Christine hired a retired senior public servant to spend some time evaluating the changes she was trying to implement. We find that many women, after attending our programs, invite us into their organisations to do the same thing—to act as credible catalysts, to direct attention to reforms that may be languishing, to give momentum and visibility to important issues.

Identify and respond to what else is going on, or 'externalise the conflict'

One of the common risks leaders encounter is when public or organisational attention is focused on them rather than on the issue or reform they are working on. It's a risk that particularly women face, as public debate starts to centre on their character or their qualifications to lead. We have seen it in many political campaigns, including the lead-up to the 2016 US presidential election, which we discussed earlier. How can women leaders deal with this?

Drawing on the 1984 American vice-presidential campaign of Geraldine Ferraro, Ron Heifetz argues that while being ostensibly criticised for her husband's financial affairs, Ferraro did not see or ignored the fact that the real issue she was coming up against was about her being a woman seeking to be the Vice President. Heifetz recommends that we need to first recognise that a woman as Vice President 'posed a major adaptive challenge to men and women throughout the land'.[5] Then he advises that the leader put effort into 'externalising the conflict'—that is, directing it back to the bigger issues at hand.

Our view is that this is a very complex risk and there are no simple strategies to respond when leadership gets personal, as it particularly does for women, and for women who are pioneers. Some commentators suggest that as Australia's first woman Prime Minister Julia Gillard waited too long to respond to the personal criticisms that were undermining her leadership—such as financial arrangements for renovations to a house, or the 'empty fruit bowl' seen in her kitchen in a magazine article that conveyed, to some, lack of heart and compassion as a woman, or her clothes. Behind these attacks were two issues that she later directly addressed: her legitimacy to be Prime Minister due to her predecessor being ousted by their party and her role in that, and being Australia's first female Prime Minister. In both Ferraro's and Gillard's case they eventually called out and dealt with these issues.

These responses, though, drew a lot of criticism too. Gillard, though widely applauded in the international media for her 'misogyny speech', was roundly criticised in the Australian press for 'playing the gender card'. As we have described elsewhere and have both adopted, one approach is to be upfront about our gender and our identification as women, to pre-empt gendered criticisms, and be clear that we will support other women because it is right and fair, and because it will make for enhanced outcomes.

Reduce reactivity to criticism and attacks

In her leadership, Christine has experienced a lot of resistance, as well as personally directed attacks and publicly aired criticism. Handling such resistance and criticism often involves several overlapping strategies.

The first is to recognise that resistance is a predictable response to something you have to do as part of your role. Many of the actions and decisions made by leaders provoke strong reactions. In the many situations where Christine faced strong pushback or resistance, it helped her to remind herself that her role required her to make decisions that people might not agree with. It's the role—not you personally—that they are reacting to. In a particular example, she remembers deciding to implement a policy in Victoria Police that no alcohol was to be stored or drunk on police premises. The policy was backed by research and by Victoria Police's management team in order to deal with a problem of excessive alcohol consumption by police, with all the known consequences for the health and wellbeing of other police, the families of members and the community.

A Commissioner's Instruction was distributed to all employees. Despite a wave of complaint, often directed personally, that this was a time-honoured way of police dealing with the stress of the job, that drinks on Fridays or at the end of shifts helped teams bond, Christine knew that this policy change was vital. The research and evidence were clear. She implemented the policy and was responsible for it, but never took the outrage personally. She also excluded suspect persons from casinos around Australia during the time of the underworld murders. The letter the suspect persons received informing them about the ban was from Christine, but in her role as Chief Commissioner.

Second, Christine recommends leaders ask from whom the criticism is coming and whether those individuals should be listened to and given credence. Elaborating on this strategy, Christine says:

> If you have a public profile and are being criticised, you don't need to beat yourself up about comments from people you don't know and probably don't respect. Of course, take notice of those you respect, but don't let strangers undermine you. Remember that some radio and online commentators are paid and rewarded to make inflammatory comments. The more outrageous, the more attention. There are built-in incentives for them to exaggerate. An example of this is when a talk-show host rang up and threatened to play a tape of me on air closing the Armed Offenders Squad. The commentator was trumpeting it as the end of my career. I knew what I had said and was happy to call the radio announcer's bluff, telling him to play the tape. The issue fizzled and members of the public largely supported my stand to take decisive action. If a criticism is based on facts or evidence and comes from a reputable source then listen, and respond, if it is just opinion, then take it or leave it. Make it your business to know where valuable commentary is likely to come from— the journalists who know their material, the academics whose research you trust and who are more likely to come from an impartial, reasoned perspective. These are the views to listen to.

A third strategy is to simply screen out the clutter of public commentary. Don't listen to the radio, read newspapers and websites selectively and don't go trawling for bad commentaries.

Finally, Christine recommends keeping a sense of humour and perspective:

> Over time I have developed a more generous capacity to laugh at myself and to help others do the same. On occasions, I have been asked to give speeches and to please make sure I'm 'funny'. I got a card recently from a client who thanked me for being inspiring and funny. Looking for the lighter side in a situation and being able to convey it to others helps all of us cope with the inevitable upsets and setbacks.

Know why you're doing it—be clear and connected to purpose

When things get tough it's very useful to remind yourself of the value you are creating or the importance of the work to the community, organisation, team or individuals. We hear many stories about how small things leaders or teachers said and did dramatically and positively changed another's path.

Take the time to remind yourself about why you are committed to your profession or industry. What were the values that inspired you? Sometimes reiterating values or purpose can be seen as sentimental or we can retreat to cynicism about the perversion of values we see. For Amanda, her belief that education should be about freeing and empowering others has been a touchstone and a check. There have been times when she has felt that she was caught up in academic processes that don't support this purpose. At those times, she has sought to step back and make changes in what she was doing to better align with why she is in higher education. Gillard says that throughout the three years of her prime ministership, it was her determination to reform educational and disability opportunities that kept her focused and allowed her to screen out the taunts and machinations of political life.

Part of staying connected to purpose is to remind yourself of achievements—not in an egocentric way but just to remind you of what matters and the difference you have made. This might be an organisational or group activity. For several years after the 2009 Victorian bushfires, reports were prepared on the progress to recovery, initially daily, then monthly, then three-monthly, and then annually. These reports kept a large group focused and confident of improvement despite the huge challenges. At a more individual level, this might be about keeping thank-you cards or letters, or stepping back to create a scorecard of your achievements. We keep score in sports because we want to know who wins. Consider developing your version of a scorecard, not a résumé but a record of those outcomes you're proud of: changes implemented, problems solved, individuals helped, awards received—things that confirm for you that you are worth it and have done some great things.

Change how you feel (and think) about fear

Leadership is laden with difficult situations. It is human and normal to feel fear when tackling an issue that needs action, when addressing a group that may seek to undermine or sabotage you, in pushing back and questioning the directive of someone more senior.

There are several key things we can all do to cope with fear better. They don't involve making the fear go away but they do involve changing our mental and emotional relationship to it:

- understand that everyone feels fear and don't judge yourself for it

- assess as calmly and coolly as you can the risks, sometimes drawing on confidantes who are both supportive and honest

- ask yourself what the thinking is behind your fears—how much catastrophising is adding fuel to your feelings? Do you have old habits of fearing something that you don't need to reactivate anymore? (For more on the mind's role in creating fear see our earlier discussion of 'the impostor syndrome' in chapter 9 and the next chapter's discussion of mindfulness and resilience.)

We are far more afraid than we need to be. Christine has asked herself, 'What's the worst thing they can do to me? Shoot me? That's very unlikely.'

Value other sides of yourself, and know when to move on

Often, we stay in a relationship, job, community or organisation for too long. Change is hard and making a move can sometimes come with losses that feel unbearable. In Christine's work in leading changes in family violence, she saw many women stay fruitlessly in damaging relationships. Women hope for a change in their partner's behaviour, believe there is nowhere else to go, or are afraid to leave because of fear of retribution from their partner (research shows this fear to be well founded, as leaving is the most dangerous time for women).

In work situations, we stay too long because of pressure from within and without. Others say, 'Don't leave—we need you', 'We still have much work to do' or 'What will we do without you?' Internally we may be afraid to consider what's next—'Who will hire me?' 'This is the only thing I know how to do.' 'What will I do with my days?' The strange thing about these behaviours is that to everything in life there is a beginning, a middle and an end. Somehow, we just don't want to see the signs that it's time to leave or make a change—and on some occasions we ignore the signs to our own detriment.

In February 2008, Christine returned to work after a holiday and was given a gift by a younger member of the executive team. The book was *The Hero's Farewell: What happens when CEOs retire* by Jeffery Sonnenfeld, and it tracked the journeys to retirement or departure of several CEOs. As Christine describes it:

> It started me thinking that the time to leave was approaching. By 2008 I was seeing strong signs of change in the organisation. I had been involved in appointing 95 per cent of the top

200 leaders. We had come through corruption challenges and underworld murders, settled enterprise bargains, reduced crime and death on the roads, reconnected with our communities and much more. I said to myself, it's time to go. I discussed the departure with the minister, who suggested I was on a roll and should stay a few years longer. He asked me to stay on with another three-year contract. Eventually, in November 2008, after a round of criticism about a trip I took with my husband to the United States, I called and invited the minister to the announcement of my departure. I invited the senior executive to a meeting the same morning, advising them of my decision. I then announced it to the organisation and the community. I was encouraged to stay until my replacement was announced, hopefully in February 2009.

As it turned out, my plans and hopes were overtaken by the terrible Victorian bushfires in 2009. As Police Commissioner, I was also Emergency Chief at that time—an arrangement that has since been changed. Shortly after the fires the premier asked me to take on the very important job of overseeing the Victorian Bushfire Reconstruction and Recovery Authority—a role that would fully engage and stretch me for several more years.

The points I want to make by quoting these experiences are to trust your instincts, to not fear change and to make sure you keep developing yourself and a range of interests so that you are not staying in an unsustainable role out of fear or lack of an alternative.

Leadership programs such as the ones we run can provide space or discussion for women to make big positive career, and sometimes life changes. Participants see themselves with fresh eyes, recognising talents and values that they and their current colleagues take for granted or devalue. The result is that they feel more confident to 'put themselves out there'. As Christine says, she applied for several senior jobs and got rejected before she was successful in Victoria. With hindsight, those rejections were good things!

To make changes and be open to new paths ensures that your work doesn't define you. Seek out and value relationships that have nothing to do with your role but through which you get a sense of support and worth. Christine and Amanda have both pursued outside interests that provide a change of pace but also bring a sense of being able to contribute in wider ways. For Christine, in 2002 it was the purchase of a property within a two-hour drive of Melbourne. She and John moved their Clydesdale horses from New South Wales and found an environment and community in which to decompress, refresh and renew. She also took up mosaics, an interest she has pursued ever since.

For Amanda, becoming a yoga and then meditation teacher provided an energising and hopeful path when she felt burned out from her role as a business school professor. The experience changed her sense of herself and how she could be a positive influence in the world in a different way from how she had always thought of herself. An unexpected benefit was bringing the learning from that experience into her teaching and research, enabling her to be more courageous and let other pressures go past.

13
Resilience and renewal

> *Human beings have enormous resilience.*
>
> Muhammad Yunus

How can women exercise innovative and effective leadership in organisations and communities but do so without significant cost to their health and happiness or to that of those around them? This is an important question for all leaders. Finding a different or more sustainable way to do leadership is a common reason many women come to our programs. There is substantial evidence that work experienced as unrelenting, largely out of our control or requiring decisions that go against our sense of what's right often elicits profound consequences for our mental and physical health, as well as our day-to-day ability to enjoy and adapt to circumstances.

There is no single, simple answer to supporting leaders on these issues, though there has been a lot of research, for example, on cultivating resilience. Some organisations have invested in wellness programs, such as stress management or yoga classes. These efforts can be seen in two ways: as welcome initiatives, where senior management recognise the importance of supporting their employees to be healthy; or, more critically, as efforts to mask fundamentally unsustainable work practices, such as routinely requiring very long working hours.[1] Both responses may be valid. The important point for us is that everyone's circumstances are unique and individuals need time and encouragement to explore how they can flourish in their leadership. Ask yourself:

- What are the signs for me that things are out of balance?

- What are the non-negotiables in life that I need to live well and that can't be compromised?

- What activities and routines enable me to feel empowered and energised in my work?

- How can I model and lead generative and life-affirming work cultures?

We offer several different ideas, practices and strategies that our experience has shown are valuable to individuals working in high-pressure or demanding roles. Our message is not that you must hang in there no matter what. It's to step back and take time to assess what's important. It's to back your own intuition about what makes you happy and fulfilled. It's to exercise self-care and compassion towards yourself, putting a value on enjoying life rather than feeling you have no option or must endure—as we outline in chapter 12, this involves cultivating interests and activities outside your job that help you feel you have choices. We draw on our observations and the writings of other women, as well as research on coping with stress, mindfulness and resilience. But the only important criterion is whether these approaches are helpful to you in making decisions and trade-offs about your career and how you exercise leadership.

Stress—its causes and some responses

All of us experience tragedies and setbacks, when we doubt we can carry on. Yet the evidence is that it is not these events that cause us debilitating stress, with all its array of psychological and physiological consequences, but the way we think about those events. Understanding some of the emerging research and insights about stress and its causes can offer solutions.

Stress occurs for many of us when circumstances outstrip our resources and capacities to respond and cope.[2] Research has shown that brief bursts of very difficult or demanding circumstances are rarely in themselves bad for us. So long as they don't last too long and we have a sense of having weathered them in decent shape, this kind of time-limited, endurable stress can give us a sense of our strength and resilience.

What is bad for us is when we experience those challenging circumstances as ongoing and out of our control. In these situations, our bodies keep producing fight-or-flight response hormones, such as cortisol, and other bodily markers of stress like an elevated heart rate and increasing inflammation. The pattern of response to such an extended experience—after perhaps an additional boost to alertness and performance—is fatigue, illness, exhaustion and possibly breakdown of some sort. In some cases, where individuals stay in a very challenged state, they develop a kind of hypervigilance, where issues and people around them start to be seen as potential threats. They become used to—even addicted to—life at this feverish edge.

In two large American studies reported by stress researcher Kelly McGonigal, people who experienced a lot of overt stress but viewed it as bearable or survivable experienced the best outcomes in terms of health and longevity.[3] In contrast, others died or suffered from the belief that their stress was bad for them. It wasn't the objective circumstance that determined health and life outcomes but how people thought about them. McGonigal admits that these findings fly against many of her early research career beliefs and assumptions about stress. However, she is now on a mission to help people to reframe many physiological responses to stress as potentially helpful, creating what she calls a 'biology of courage' and a functional response of reaching out to others when things feel tough.

How can we respond differently in a potentially stressful scenario? Research tells us that it is our thoughts and our bodies that hold keys. First, we need to notice and unwind patterns of excessive or 'over' thinking; that is, being captured in ruminative and catastrophising thought patterns. When we are already operating under challenge, it is helpful to notice if we are doing a lot of 'rehearsing'—about what further can go wrong—and 'rehashing'—going over and over difficult events with a lot of blaming and self-judgement.

Second, our bodies can often help us alter these thinking patterns, for example, through slowing down, breathing more deeply or encouraging ourselves to physically relax. Since Harvard researcher Howard Benson discovered the power of the 'relaxation response' in the 1970s, a wide range of other evidence has shown how powerful it is to allow our body to relax. Some maintain that it is our natural condition. We don't need to go anywhere special to get it but rather just turn our minds down and let the body do what comes naturally.

Research also shows, though, that many of us have lost or had conditioned out of us the capacity to relax or let go of things that may seem urgent but are not all that important. For those of us in this category—and there are increasing numbers due to our 'always on' societies and roles with expectations of 24-hour mobile and email availability—we may need to structure in relaxation opportunities: times for walks or exercise, attending yoga or tai chi classes, regular meditation or listening to music, gardening, cycling, cooking.

Though we are describing here ways of managing work-related stress, the approaches of meditation, yoga and relaxation have also been used in more extreme situations of chronic illness and post-traumatic stress disorder (PTSD). Learning such practices doesn't take away these conditions, but there is substantial evidence that it helps people deal with symptoms better, with corresponding improvements in indicators of physical health and psychological wellbeing.

One way to deal with feelings of stress is therefore to understand how it is caused and find alternative ways to respond. While the evidence is that moderate amounts of challenge are good for us, energising and promoting high performance, a semi-permanent state of hypervigilance is bad for both our performance and our health. Noticing when we have moved into this state, or become 'hooked' on it, opens the door to us making a choice about whether we stay or find ways out of a hyperalert state.

Resilience

There has been a lot of psychological research and many books focused on helping people be resilient. We take the view that resilience is not about steeling yourself to survive or bounce back from damaging or unsustainable roles and organisational cultures. Resilience for us is less a personality trait than being practical and preventative—approaches everyone can adopt. It is about taking steps to reduce the risks that can be faced in leadership, as described in chapter 12. It is about developing habits of seeking advice, asking for help and acting on good information. Resilience is about making choices and taking agency and not leaving your health, wellbeing or living conditions in the hands of others. It is about valuing, making time and planning for your physical, emotional and financial wellbeing.

In her role as Chair of Good Shepherd Microfinance, Christine has learned about and increasingly become an advocate for women's financial resilience. Research shows that women are much more vulnerable financially, likely to have less superannuation and fewer financial options in older age, more likely to live in poverty. The principles that apply in fostering financial resilience also apply in other areas of life: valuing yourself and your rights to happiness and independence; cultivating friendships, connections and activities that support you and reinforce that you make a difference to others; sharing issues with trusted others and seeking help if you are feeling isolated or in doubt.

During turbulent experiences and often while under personal attack, Christine has developed the following ways to be resilient.

Have a sense of humour

Laugh at yourself and the situation. There have been cartoonists who have filled news pages with less than flattering, but often insightful drawings of and about me. I have collected some and they hang proudly in my home office.

Maintain energy and flow

During my time in the police and with the Bushfire Recovery Authority, I worked hard—often seven days a week. The adrenaline and the sense of urgency and purpose sustained me beyond what I could have imagined. I learned, though, that this can only go on for a limited time and then you should back off. I remember being in Daylesford to meet a community to talk about the fires. I lost my voice as I commenced the meeting, and others in the team took over. It took me some weeks to recover.

Know that you have coped before and will again

It is important to 'layer' your leadership. By this I mean to recognise that each experience adds to your knowledge and toolbox of skills. Draw strength from this and the fact that you survived last time and will again.

Take consolation from your achievements

Many years ago, I came to understand that I would need to account for my work—that I needed to be able to say to the doubters, 'This is what I/the team/region/organisation have/has achieved'. This habit has always stood me in good stead. While managing the Human Resources and Education Department in the NSW Police Service from 1994 to 1997, and after the Wood Royal Commission into Corruption in the NSW Police, police members did groundbreaking work. We were often challenged as to what we had achieved, but we kept data, met deadlines and used a detailed program management approach that we could call upon to respond to the cynics, showing real evidence of our work. I continued with the same data management at Victoria Police and the Bushfire Authority.

Personally, I also kept a scorecard of my achievements—not quite a résumé but a checklist so that when things get tough I could look at it and think, 'Yes, I have achieved much'. It helped me ignore the negative comments.

Don't become 'one of the boys' or someone you're not

Often, we adopt behaviours to fit in, to go with the flow. Sometimes it could be because it's just easier to go along to get on; other times it is because we like the new person we become. In chapter 10, we discuss how and why some women relinquish a sense of being women. When I was a younger police officer, some policewomen cut their hair in a boyish fashion, wore male-style shirts and developed a swagger. I found myself drinking much more and swearing after I'd been in operational policing for a while. I remember one day finding myself in a pub at 6 a.m. drinking beer and thinking, 'I've had enough. I don't care if they don't like me—I'm not doing this anymore.' Much to my surprise, when I announced I wasn't going drinking after work anymore, no one in the team cared. I was also told the only way to get ahead in policing was to join the Freemasons or learn to play golf. One was not possible and the other I rejected.

We are all different. There is often a personal and psychological cost of fitting in—we give up who we are. There are enough men already and we don't need women pretending to be men!

Pick your battles

With apologies to singer Kenny Rogers, you need to know when to hold, when to fold and when to run. His song 'The Gambler' contains good advice to choose the battles you take on. Some are too dangerous to tackle and, as Heifetz also suggests, you can become a martyr or get done over, losing hard-earned credibility. As any cricketer knows, you cannot hit all the balls. You might let some go through to the keeper. Wait till the timing is right and know then that you can make a difference.

Understand the rules

In work and organisations there are always stated and unstated rules. Pay attention to them and decide if and how you want to abide by them. When still relatively junior in the NSW Police, I found myself Chair of the Women's Branch of the NSW Police Association. Having no idea of how to chair or the rules of the Association, I obtained a copy the Police Association Rules then bought a book that explained meeting procedures. It didn't take much study but it was all I needed. Do the work to understand the processes or systems that will help you achieve your goals.

Find a supportive partner

Research and my experience strongly back the notion that many women who succeed have a supportive partner. Often all we see is another side: the pressure women are under to fulfil their many roles of wife, partner, mother, daughter, colleague and friend. I tackle this issue directly with the many groups of women I work with. Things often get very quiet at the point when I suggest that many women don't have support for their work from their spouses. In some cases, they are subjected to emotional, physical, sexual and financial abuse or manipulation by their intimate partner. Our advice then is to seek help, talk to trusted friends about what to do, go to websites to seek out information. Leaving these relationships is very hard and at times dangerous, but it is possible. After these class discussions, some women talk about how things change in their relationship. One young woman spoke of a shared decision to buy her retired partner a boat so that he would stop trying to run her life. Another said that her partner finally made lists and did his bit at home.

'Bobbing about' or 'having a go'

In 2007, Victoria Police managed security for the FINA World Swimming Championships. The opening ceremony saw each of the competing countries introduced, their national anthem played and then a float of their country's flag placed in the pool at which most of the events were held. The ceremony was long and I took to watching the floats as they bobbed around in the pool, drifting about with the flow. The following day, I went back to the pool for the competition swimming—some swimmers won, others were not so good and some swam their personal best. All got in at one end and swam determinedly towards the other.

It illustrated for me the choices people and organisations make—they can just 'bob about' with no real direction, not sure of where they are going, or be like the swimmers that dived into the water and had a go. I have worked for organisations that had no idea what they wanted to achieve; rather, they just bobbed about looking very busy. People can also be like this, bumped around with no real plan or idea of what they want or any focus for their lives. The question I ask is: Which are you—the float reacting to random currents or the swimmer?

Respect yourself

We have all done things we regret. We've behaved badly, drunk too much, had relationships we wished we hadn't, said things we cannot take back—that's life. The real question is: Can you live with it or does it do you harm? If you can live with it, forgive yourself and move on. If it's causing you ongoing grief, think about making amends, apologising or seeking help to make changes.

Renewal

In 2004, Amanda published an article called 'Renewal' that described a crisis point in her career, when she realised she needed to step back from what felt like an unsustainable role as an academic professor.[4] It wasn't just that she felt she had no time to give to the things that mattered—she felt she wasn't showing any leadership in her own life and work, and that she had lost connection with her values and why she had become a teacher and academic. All her energies were being spent on the wrong things.

The article she wrote describes how taking a year off to finish her yoga teacher training enabled her to renew herself—to return to a different mix of teaching, researching and leadership with 'fresh eyes', appreciative of her students, colleagues and the opportunities her environment and professorial role presented.

Amanda has found that it is this article, which is written in a personal way, rather than other more academic ones, that strikes a chord with leaders. They recognise themselves in it, especially in the checklist of behaviours that may signal the need for renewal (see checklist). It's an exercise worth doing. As Amanda was writing and reviewing this in 2016, she was aware of repeating some of those patterns. Maybe more renewal is needed!

Checklist to work out whether you need some renewal—or where Amanda was at in 2001

1. Getting up earlier, staying at work later and using the weekend to check and process emails.

2. Can't have friends over on the weekend because you use the time for recovery from the previous week and preparation for next.

3. Don't have long phone calls to friends who are far away.

4. Can't remember when you last read a novel for pure pleasure; always taking textbooks or work-related reading matter to bed.

5. Hardly ever sit down and eat together as a family with the TV off.

6. Find it hard to put aside work thoughts when you are talking to your kids or partner, difficulty being 'completely present'.

7. Find that unless you schedule it in and make a determined effort, you go for long periods without talking to your family (parents, siblings).

8. Consciously have to make appointment time for sex, and these times become rarer.

9. Feel deprived and 'hard done by' a fair bit of the time, with a sense of martyrdom creeping in.

We all need to gain perspective, and sometimes this means giving ourselves permission for renewal. It can take different forms and, in our experience, there is often more opportunity than we think to negotiate for some renewal time from our organisation or employer.

In other circumstances, we might need to give ourselves permission to make radical changes, to leave familiarity and back ourselves along a new path. One example comes from an ANZSOG Women in Leadership program we taught recently. The participants were senior public sector executives from all around Australia and New Zealand. Though a small group, they were very diverse in terms of their experience and sector, from very senior federal government officials to younger women with little public sector experience but a lot of life experience. Tentative at first, many assumed they should just listen because others knew much more. Some experienced individuals were also being careful not to crowd out others. It was one of the most experienced women in the room who, in revealing a lot about some challenging organisational circumstances she was enduring, helped the group get very real and start to listen to, and connect with, each other at a deeper level despite their differences. It doesn't always happen but when it does, this contextual shift to greater openness and learning is wonderful to experience. What it does is help others get out of their business-as-usual thinking.

The reason for dwelling on this particular program is that there were several women who made big renewal decisions afterwards. Amanda spoke with one senior bureaucrat over breakfast. It turned out that this leader, who was recognised as being smart and successful, had a fascinating background and set of interests that had been 'parked' in her current role. Her colleagues knew nothing of them and she routinely delivered only a small part of the value she could offer—albeit very effectively. She communicated with us six months after completing the program to say she had made a big change—of country and role as it turned out—and was feeling very empowered and confident about her ability to make a difference with more of herself 'in play'. Another participant stepped up to reshape the direction and momentum of her agency. She did this uninvited and unasked, initially by simply raising some new possibilities that we had explored in the program, and then inviting Christine to come and work with senior executives.

What sits behind these examples is the recognition that many of us have more energies, commitments and capabilities—more sides to us—some of which have been put on hold or tamped down because we may have met with resistance or felt the need to fit in. Finding ways to step back often reminds us of these parts of ourselves. It can give us the energy and the courage to back ourselves for new or bigger challenges, and with a wider repertoire of resilient responses if things don't go perfectly.

Mindfulness

Over the last ten or so years, Amanda has been introducing ideas and practices of mindfulness into her work with leaders, her teaching and coaching. She has found that of all the concepts and theories she draws on, it is often mindfulness that is most useful to people in their work.

Mindfulness is the very simple act of choosing to be present and aware in the moment, observing thoughts rather than getting caught up with them as necessarily reality or the truth. To be mindful is to bring body and mind to the same place—a large study by Harvard researchers shows that almost 70 per cent of the time, our mind and body are in different places. Yet people feel happier and more effective when their mind is with their body and on the people, issues and tasks with them at that moment. Support for this idea also comes from high-performance research, which documents that musicians and sportspeople who are 'in the flow' and not with their minds elsewhere perform their best. While there are many myths about mindfulness—that you must retreat to a cave in silence to do it—it is valuable to distinguish mindfulness from meditation. Meditation is the process of sitting with focused attention, yet mindfulness is a choice to be present now and can be applied in all our daily activities—having conversations, juggling priorities, encouraging others. That's why it is so well suited to leadership.

There is a substantial amount of neuroscientific research and cognitive science that shows how these effects work, including how practising mindfulness changes brain physiology, which in turn supports increased capacity to reduce reactivity and distractedness, improving our ability to focus and pay attention to what matters.[5]

How can cultivating mindfulness help in leadership? In Amanda's work with leaders, three ideas and practices seem particularly valuable:

1. Practise mindful listening or consciously decide to turn down internal narratives—the assessing and judging—commentary

while listening in conversation or meetings. With quite a small amount of practice, most of us can notice how much of this internal narrative is going on and how much we are not hearing because of it. We can also patiently bring ourselves back to offering our whole selves in the service of listening from stillness.[6] Sometimes people complain, 'Oh, I've got to jump in to be heard—that's how it works in my organisation.' But an enormous amount of this jumping in is not heard. It's just everyone waiting for a gap. So, the possibility of really listening can be a powerful leadership intervention that models values of respect and genuine inclusion to others.

2. Help people understand and make a distinction between modes of mind, such as thinking, reflecting and mindful awareness. The evidence is that 'excessive thinking' (as described above) is not good for us. Yet most of us over-rely on thinking. All of us are able to bring more than our thinking to work and leadership. Further, our value as leaders is more likely to be in our capacity to pay and direct attention, reflect and take perspective, than in our capacity to solve an immediate problem or provide a technical fix. Again, with quite a small amount of mindful practice, we can begin noticing that we are thinking—repetitively or ruminatively—and that that pattern of thinking isn't solving anything. With that recognition comes the possibility of choosing where the mind goes, perhaps just for the next few moments. As an example, we can invite the mind to notice that that's where it's been, or we can allow ourselves to be aware of the day or the people around us. We can draw on the physical senses to help us relax and enjoy life instead of rushing headlong through it.

3. Mindfulness provides a means of noticing ego, and guidance on how to move towards practising leadership with less ego. In Amanda's own experience, this has been a very valuable

idea, especially in difficult situations or with potentially resistant or hostile audiences, when her ego is getting over-involved. The signs are that she is feeling defensive, not listening, stereotyping the audience, ready with a comeback. Buddhist conceptions of mindfulness remind us that the selves we so often busily protect and defend are just aspects of ego. Many aspects of the self—what views we hold, what we think we need or deserve—are just a set of constructed narratives that can get in the way of us being effective and courageous in leadership. While working hard for valuable causes is usually worthwhile, it is almost always better to pursue those ends with less attachment to ourselves and our ego.

14

Wise words from women

> *The knowledge of women ... is what allows women to struggle for freedom without being co-opted by false pretensions or by the brute exertions of power for its own sake.*
>
> Jacqueline Rose, 2014

Throughout this book, we have suggested that despite women exercising leadership in diverse and innovative ways, their contribution has often been neglected or cast as something other than leadership, because it is women who are doing it. In this final chapter, we draw together what we have learned from listening to, reading and watching women leaders.

The content comes from several sources. As part of running Women in Leadership programs, we have had the opportunity to hear a wide range of senior women talking openly and candidly about their experiences and journeys—the failures and setbacks as well as the successes. These women have been dinner speakers and panellists, and their advice and responses to questions are distilled here. They have not always agreed, and they have gone about their leadership and building their careers in diverse ways. We also include here some of what we have learned from women over the course of our studies and careers about the obstacles to women and how to go about changing societies and organisations to uphold the rights of women and girls and build respectful and inclusive societies.

'Many paths up the mountain'

In terms of planning and advancing careers, the women we have learned from cover the full gamut. At one very successful extreme are those who have taken a 'whole of career' perspective, planning a long way ahead and identifying roles and the experience they need to get there. At the other extreme are some equally successful opportunists who have stretched themselves to step up and meet challenges for which they often felt unprepared. Several of our panellists have admitted they 'didn't have a plan' and were 'not driven to be number one'. Rather, as one senior New Zealand bureaucrat described it, 'What got me out of bed was delivering valuable things through and for people.'

In between the two extremes are those who have applied and been rejected for leadership roles, and who have applied again. As one woman described it, 'Be careful about what you get hung up about. There are many paths up the mountain. It's still the same moon at the top.' The point here is not to compare yourself to others or expect you have to achieve via a certain route.

Believe in yourself and be yourself

In her book *Gravity* about Julia Gillard's period as Australian Prime Minister, author Mary Delahunty asks Gillard, 'Did you feel you could really be yourself as PM?' She replies, 'You can be yourself, but always with a bit of padding on.'[1]

There is no one right way to build a leadership career, but the advice of most women is to not wait around for your talent to be recognised by bosses, selection panels or mentors—that may never occur. In a forum on female leadership in the public sector in November 2015, a group of senior women bureaucrats described the process of doing this: 'Find and understand your own unique "kernel of confidence" and let it flourish.'[2] Backing yourself sometimes involves being bold and venturing out beyond your confidence and competence limits.

A New Zealand panellist said, 'Put yourself on a ledge. Do things that are scary, that you don't know whether you can.'

Believing in yourself also includes trusting your instincts—about people and issues—and being clear about your values, what you will and won't do. Although the evidence is that women are judged more harshly for their confidence or ambition, the advice of a departmental secretary was, 'You don't have to become some kind of ball-breaking, arse-kicking bastard, just be confident, calm, know your stuff and be prepared to get out there and do it. And just do not succumb to the stereotypes.' Christine sometimes quotes Oscar Wilde saying, 'Be yourself. Everyone else is taken.'

Also, be willing to be different. At a recent event at which Christine spoke, an information technology executive panellist arrived in a bright, sparkling outfit. Others remarked that it encouraged them to go away and wear what they wanted—to not hold back or stay in camouflage. Another woman volunteered that she had been unemployed for eighteen months—a brave thing to do in a forum about leadership careers. She gave advice on what to do in her situation and the importance of healing. She had brushed up on French, opened an invitation-only restaurant on her balcony, and run a marathon. She used the time to renew, to reacquaint with herself and passions outside work that had lain dormant. But her message was also not to wait till redundancy to do this.

Another way for women to honour their difference is to lead with heart as well as head. Some maintain, as we have in this book, that tuning into one's own and others' emotions is not a sign of weak leadership but a vital source of intelligence.[3] Being prepared to acknowledge your own and others' feelings may be necessary for leaders in particular circumstances. Some communities and organisations are waiting for just such an acknowledgement of shared feelings from leaders in order to begin healing or changing. In these circumstances 'wearing your heart on your sleeve' is a very good thing to do. Leadership research shows it is the link between the heart and the head that people follow: if we demonstrate that others matter to us, we will matter to them.

Understand the challenges of being one of few women at senior levels

A long tradition of research, starting with Rosabeth Moss Kanter's pioneering 1977 book *Men and Women of the Corporation*, documents that women leaders, especially in traditionally male-dominated organisations, are singled out as tokens. They experience high visibility and are often isolated or have their behaviour judged as emblematic of all women.

How do women leaders cope with this? First, they focus on their achievements and track record—as Christine has suggested, they keep score of criteria that matter. Second, they remind us to recognise that these are dynamics of systems that all 'minorities' encounter.

It is valuable to understand that reactions are not about the individual and that we should avoid adding an extra layer of self-criticism to such experiences. 'You will be criticised. Take it seriously, not personally,' says one senior bureaucrat. Gillard's time as Australia's Prime Minister is a study in this. Amanda's reflections on reading Julia Gillard's *My Story* and coping with sexist attacks:

> Many of us who watched Julia Gillard's prime ministership closely were even more keen to hear her views after she lost the leadership to Kevin Rudd and moved on from politics—as she promised she would do. We weren't disappointed. In her interviews and writing she loosened up, letting her humour, perceptiveness and graciousness through, which had seemed so tightly bottled when she was in office. In her book she covers many issues, but the ones we found most insightful are her reflections on the role gender played in her leadership. She says that when she began as PM she made a decision not to make much of being the first woman in the role, hoping that the sexist and gendered references would subside, 'then peter out. I was wrong. [They] actually worsened.'[4]
>
> Once she realised that she would be attacked and undermined as a woman, her next challenge was how to

respond to this. She recalls, 'Of all the experiences I had as Prime Minister, gender is the hardest to explain, to catch, to quantify ... if you point to specific examples they sound trivial; talk more broadly and there are counter examples.'[5] So, initially at least she just ignored the stereotyping, the abusive commentaries about her appearance, her childlessness, her lack of—or alternatively too emotional—reactions. The then Opposition Leader, Tony Abbott, used phrases publicly that had long been associated with putting women down, such as 'Are you suggesting that when it comes to Julia Gillard, "no" doesn't mean "no"?' and 'If the PM wants to make an honest woman of herself, she needs to seek a mandate'. Gillard found that despite her position, the language and images attached to her were those of rape and prostitution.

Finally, and some say belatedly, Gillard struck back with her internationally renowned 'misogyny speech', in which she named the sexism to which she and other Australian women had been subject. It was a key moment for Gillard and one that earned her enormous respect from women and men around the globe, though both the local media and the Opposition argued predictably that she was 'playing the victim card'. She concluded that she couldn't ignore gender or the gender attacks, she simply had to develop a sense of self and self-worth that was independent of the media.

Be reflective and resilient

Women leaders encounter many significant structural and cultural barriers, but other barriers are primarily in our heads. These are the recurring internal narratives, self-talk and judgements, such as 'I can't do that' or 'I'm useless because I didn't get that job'. Understand where you come from and what your tendencies are under pressure. Notice the temptation to feel 'it's all about me'. Pushback and resistance from others are more likely to be about what you represent, whether it's change or a departure from the familiar.

When experiencing knockbacks, leaders advise that you first need to recognise that it hurts and, if it helps, allow yourself 'a big cry'. Then be observant about and manage your stress levels—especially noticing the effects of prolonged pressure: Are you consistently self-medicating or overindulging in alcohol? Use the support of a good team and make choices about how many social events you'll attend. Most leaders establish rules or habits to protect themselves that are not inviolate—they can be overruled under extreme circumstances. Planning regular holidays, avoiding working all weekend, having exercise routines and other ways to 'check out' are all part of re-nourishing. Many leaders emphasise the importance of self-compassion and forgiveness. If you make a mistake, recognise it, do what you can to fix it, forgive yourself and move on. Finding tenderness for yourself rather than judgement or harshness is central. One leader advised to 'imagine yourself as a little kid' and bring that understanding and nurturance to yourself.

A final element of self-reflection is avoiding martyrdom, or noticing when you are sucked into an unhealthy self-narrative of being punished or suffering. This may require strategies of 'turning off the internal chatter', stepping back, getting others to step up and, in some cases, exiting. According to one leader, 'saying no can be empowering. It's okay to seek work–life balance in a way that feels right for you.'

Three principles distilled from a public sector leadership forum

1. Challenge yourself. Panellists discussed the importance of the breadth and diversity of their experience, which has enabled them to take on increasingly complex challenges and opportunities in their careers. This requires courage to move beyond personal comfort zones, to confidently claim a 'seat at the table' and take risks in pursing new roles and responsibilities. They spoke about their capacity to draw on a diversity of thought and skills in decision-making, highlighting this as the distinguishing factor in their careers.

2   Know and respect yourself. Understanding of self through professional and personal challenges, understanding your strengths and limitations and how to best use them, was identified as important in making decisions about personal development and knowing when to draw on others' skills. Loving and appreciating who you are underlies your capacity to receive and work with criticism from others, and keep perspective on personal wellbeing. Panellists encouraged participants to be kind to themselves and to let go of the false idea of individual 'perfection'.

3   Build resilience. Resilience was a common theme with panellists, who spoke about their resolve in tackling challenges as female leaders in male-dominated or unwelcoming working environments, leaping into new professional experiences and overcoming personal and family trials. They encouraged participants to keep up with their passions outside of work, to nurture and accept support, and to take time to re-energise and spend time with family. They also discussed the need to seek flexible working arrangements when required, and communicate with managers about personal difficulties impacting work.

Look for partners and support others

Christine observes that in any group she works with, she can immediately sense those who are supporters or potential partners. They are engaged and responsive, signalling a willingness to be part of something, and are critical supports for any leader attempting to do something new or difficult. In other situations, supporters might be outside your organisation—a 'group of angels' or old friends, a learning set, or a coach or mentor who can hold up a mirror, go to a deeper level or help you see a dynamic differently.

Many of the women leaders we have learned from have been pioneers in traditionally male-dominated environments. They have not always been supported by other women; in fact, many have been actively discouraged by the few more senior women above them. Yet consistently we also hear how other women can be of invaluable assistance to leaders, giving them the confidence to envisage a leadership career or, more practically, ensuring they get opportunities and visibility in their roles—to be seen as 'talent' by those making decisions about promotions.

This distinction—between acting as a mentor versus acting as a sponsor—is emerging as an important one in research on women's leadership careers. A colleague of ours, Jen de Vries, has undertaken extensive research, especially in policing and higher education, that shows the value of both mentors and sponsors. She defines sponsors as providing and facilitating actual jobs, visibility and opportunities, such as ensuring a woman is invited to apply or on a short list for a job. Mentors offer more general advice and encouragement based on their experience. While mentors and sponsors are great if you can get them, it's wise not to hold out for one or to believe that your success as a leader is dependent on finding one, which is a trap for some young women who see the close networks that surround male peers. It is important to remember that because they are pioneers, many women succeed without mentors or sponsors.

Further, partners, mentors and sponsors may all play their roles in subtle ways. Neither Christine nor Amanda had formal mentors or sponsors, but they did have people whose advice they could seek and trust. They had people inside and outside their organisational context who believed in them, even though they didn't agree with everything they did! For Christine, they included her father, her mother and a former commissioner of police, among many others. For Amanda, they included her partner, a senior university decision-maker, a former boss (with whom she also had many run-ins) and academic women outside her field. In hindsight, their wisdom and encouragement were pivotal.

Among the more difficult issues in leadership is the role of family, partners and spouses. Women with children sometimes feel unsupported by those without. Women without children feel their own experiences and desires for 'a life' are unheard in the focus on childcare. Sheryl Sandberg in *Lean In* advises to 'make your partner a real partner'. Negotiating adequate support at home and in elder care, or a fair division of labour in household tasks, are enormous challenges for most women in leadership. Other women may not have a partner. For those who do, as engagingly explored by Annabel Crabb in *The Wife Drought,* male leaders are rewarded for having families but protected from actually having to worry about them. Women leaders, including those in relationships where they have negotiated that their partner's career takes a back seat for a while, are judged harshly for inflicting damage on masculine pride. These difficulties are not reasons to avoid negotiating for equitable sharing of family and household responsibilities. But they are reasons to keep doing so with understanding for how hard such change can be, with compassion and self-compassion in pioneering more equitable ways forward that go against deeply socialised gender stereotypes.

Seek work that you enjoy, keep learning, affirm your talents

Keep the big picture in view and don't confuse your value with your current role. Remind yourself of your talents and interests outside work. When we have the opportunity to work with groups of women, we often enjoy a dinner together with them. Initially we invited after-dinner speakers but we realised that there were deep reserves of talent within groups that we could tap into and enjoy. We now invite women who sing, write poetry or have other talents to give performances, and we lead songs, such as the famous women's anthem 'I Am Woman'. Women are often part of vocal groups or choirs and can lead the whole group in song. Others have taught us Irish and belly dancing.

We've found that women often feel they need to keep these parts of themselves out of their formal leadership roles. Making a place for the expression of their wide experience and talents on our programs is our way of encouraging other parts of them to be 'let into' their leadership. It is also a way of recognising how much leadership is done outside formal roles. We don't need experts to tell us the answers to leadership challenges—most often we have solutions or the resources to find them within.

Recognise women's diverse experiences and work to support them to be free and to contribute

A theme among many women leaders is their recognition of the remaining significant challenges for women worldwide and their desire—through different vehicles—to work for improvements in women's rights, in education, in freedom from violence and slavery, in equal opportunity in the workplace. Women leaders see these activities as ways to contribute to wider social improvements during or after they've left formal organisational roles. Many see it as part of their responsibility, too, to make things better for the women coming after them. A starting point is often just learning more about other women's experiences and being prepared to be educated about daily reality for women and girls.

In their different spheres Amanda and Christine have become strong advocates for women. We encourage you to think about the diverse ways you can support other women. It might be an informal conversation encouraging a schoolgirl to believe in herself and aim high, or participating in international networks that foster women's business. The point here is that it's not just what you can influence in your work that's important. There are many other avenues, and we've been inspired by the diverse ways women leaders spread their impact and contribution.

The article by Christine below describes her journey of coming to a realisation of the extent of family violence, then subsequently working to change systems as part of her various roles—from policing through to now being involved in supporting women's financial independence.

> ### Ending violence against women (adapted from a newspaper article by Christine)
> Not long after I joined the police force in the 1970s, I discovered that three of my friends—all women, all police officers—were being physically abused by their husbands. All three were strong and capable women. They arrested criminals. They protected the public. They carried guns.

I was shocked. I thought if violence could touch the lives of my strong capable friends, it could touch the life of any woman. So, for the rest of my life, I have been not only aware of violence towards and abuse of women and girls, but have also worked towards solutions.

Life has changed in many ways since the 1970s, but the violence and abuse against women and girls remain with us. Seventy-one women have been murdered in 2016 alone, the majority by men who were or are their partners.

Figures collated by Australia's National Research Organisation for Women's Safety (ANROWS) paint a terrible picture of violence against women. From the age of fifteen:

- one in five Australian women experiences sexual abuse

- one in six experiences physical or sexual abuse from a current or former partner

- one in four experiences emotional abuse

- one in three experiences physical violence.

Globally, the figures for experiencing physical violence are broadly the same: one in three. That's an almost unimaginable number of one billion women.

More recently, financial abuse has been identified as an important issue. Good Shepherd Microfinance research suggests that in Australia there are two million women who have experienced financial abuse. This is a situation where the partner exercises power and control through financial means. Examples include women not being allowed to work or have credit cards, being manipulated into signing loans, or having their spending closely monitored; a husband taking out a loan in his wife's name without her knowledge; women not being allowed to have their own bank account; and women having their money transferred into their male partner's account.

The roots of this violence are attitudes that devalue and exploit women and girls, which exist throughout the world. Whether those attitudes are more common in developing countries than nations like our own is arguable. What is not arguable is that they exist. And they need to change if we are to end violence and abuse against women and girls. They need to change everywhere.

Change needs to occur at all levels of society—among individuals, among communities and among institutions. Institutional change can often seem tough, but it can certainly be done. When I joined Victoria Police, I realised that our statistics on family violence were very low when compared to my experience in New South Wales. I commissioned a major review of our response to family violence. The task force established to work on the problem came from across the police force, the community, the judiciary and a men's anti-violence group. Their combined efforts underpinned major reforms in 2004 that transformed the response to family violence across the police, the courts and our service sectors.

We have now seen a Royal Commission into Family Violence in Victoria. Violence against women is widely reported and commented on. We clearly have a long way to go but we as a society are finally talking about a crisis of violence against women and girls. As long as we treated this harm as just a family matter or a personal problem, or said it was the victim's fault, a solution was never going to be possible. Now we can work together to make a real and lasting difference.

But those billion women experiencing violence across the world need that conversation to begin where they live, too. Don't think for a moment that attitudes cannot change in developing nations. They can, and the change can make a substantial difference for women at risk of domestic violence.

An example of a project working towards change is Plan International in Uganda and Zimbabwe, which happens to be funded by the Australian government. Communities that often accepted or ignored violence against women as a fact of life saw attitudes challenged through education. While women came to understand and assert their rights, police and the courts were trained to support them. Just as in Australia, the result has been a transformation in the lives of women. Violence has not yet been eliminated, but it has been acknowledged. We need to go further—to identify the causes and condemn violence and abuse against women and girls. That's our experience in Australia, and it can and should be our experience around the world.

As this work in Africa shows, Australia has the resources to help this conversation begin at individual, community and institutional levels. But that is just a handful of communities in two countries. There are countless communities around the world—rich and poor, developed and developing—where violence against women is ignored, unacknowledged, even flourishing.

We need to export our fight against violence and abuse towards women and girls, even as we continue to wage it ourselves. Other countries have much to learn from the changes we have seen in our attitudes since I first joined the police force in the 1970s, and I daresay we have much to learn from their experiences. The conversations we have together, the leadership that women can show whatever their role or organisation, could well prove to be the keys to finally ending the scourge of violence and abuse against women and girls.

Wise women into the future

In December 2015, when Emma Watson, the *Harry Potter* actor and UN Ambassador for Women and Girls, addressed the United Nations, she made an impassioned speech about the relevance of feminism to young people. She said, 'For the record, feminism is the belief that men and women should have equal rights and opportunities. It is the theory of the political, economic and social equality of the sexes.' The speech went viral. Watson directly tackled misconceptions about feminism, inviting young women and men to align themselves with feminism and its goals.

A similarly mobilising set of moments has arisen from the otherwise deeply disappointing 2016 American election. Women including former First Lady Michelle Obama have delivered rousing calls for women to organise and support each other, to continue to push back on sexism and call out discrimination.

We feel optimistic that young women are providing powerful role models for leadership in a rapidly changing technological world, and in a political climate that threatens to erode many gains that women have made. We urge women to keep listening and learning from each other, and to keep drawing attention to and celebrating women's leadership.

Looking forward and sustaining

The questions most often asked of us at the end of programs are: 'I'm feeling inspired to lead and introduce change, but how can I maintain my enthusiasm and energy?' and 'How can I put these ideas into action, sustaining myself in the face of all the complexities and pressures of work and daily life?' We advocate both looking forward—having goals and purposes that we are committed to—and also savouring the journey. Take pleasure in what's unfolding in the present and notice that what sustains us most is often everyday interactions and the support of others.

An example of this is us writing this book together. It started out as an idea of Christine's to provide some practical advice, but the book has taken its shape over many meetings, visits and lunches. While at various times both of us have been busy with other commitments, we've relied on each other to re-enthuse with a fresh example and to energise the value of our undertaking. It has been a gift to make time, sit down together at desks and our respective dining-room tables, enjoy each other's company, share meals, as well as knowledge and ideas, and record the wisdom of women. Our message is that working with other women is sustaining—amply evidenced by our own experience.

We also encourage participants on our courses to go back and share with their teams, friends and families any changes they are seeking to make in their organisational contexts and leadership, as well as their own work habits. Some of us have a tendency to not share our desires and plans, or discount the interest others express for them. For example, when Amanda thought she might like to train as a yoga teacher, it initially felt safer to keep it to herself. She might fail, after all. But she remembers clearly the family gathering where she announced her plan to enrol in teacher training. Her family wasn't dismissive but encouraging. We have both been sustained by the responses of others when we've talked about our book: 'I'm looking forward to reading that!' they'll say. Our point here is that it is others who help us sustain effort and change—we're not alone. The key is for us to be open, share our hopes and plans, recognise the interest and support of others.

On looking forward, we have two approaches to recommend and we hope that one of them or a mix of the two might help remind you of key ideas you want to implement, ways you want to lead and to support you to do so. Both involve committing in writing what you have achieved, what you value, what you want to focus on or do more of. There is research evidence that writing—by hand rather than using a template or device—helps anchor commitment and learning.

Based on her experience as a leader wanting to embed changes, Christine comes from the 'order and structure' camp and advocates goal setting. Write down where you'll be in three months' time, what you want to achieve, and then do the same for six and twelve months. For those of you who need and respond to this kind of planning, it is a way to keep focused on what you want to change and to hold yourself accountable. One example comes from Christine's niece Amy finishing school and not being sure of what to do or where to go next. Christine set her a task to take six weeks over the Christmas break to figure out what she was going to do, and then called in to check that she had written her plan, which she had. As Christine watched over the next twelve months, this young woman started a degree and part-time work and committed to an exercise regime, which many years later she still maintains. It's become an important part of who she is and how she feels about herself. She's formulated subsequent plans. Not everything has come to fruition, but the process gave direction at a time when many young people feel aimless and flounder.

Sometimes a plan needs to involve others. One woman whose partner had recently retired needed a plan that would enable her to have freedom with less involvement (and interference!) from him. They explored goals for him that he had always wanted to pursue. She reported back that it worked.

To sustain and guide yourself into the future, Amanda recommends recording personal experiences and learning in a journal. At the end of workshops and programs, Amanda invites participants, and gives time herself, to writing a page or so addressed, 'Dear me'. Such letters are reminders about what has just unfolded. They may be statements of reassurance: that there is no need to be anxious at the start of something new, or that you can and should trust yourself, your partner and the group to co-create some valuable learning together. For Amanda there are reminders to enjoy herself and the amazing participants, and to notice and appreciate the acts of sharing, courage and risk-taking that often occur as a program unfolds.

Why write a letter to yourself? As an academic, Amanda has argued that how we write matters. Ways of writing that we employ during our work life and education often leave out the most important and influential aspects of phenomena such as how an experience felt, or how our bodies, senses and imagination were engaged.[1] There is considerable neuroscientific research that supports what novelists and great writers have always known: intelligence is embodied. What we know depends on our interactions with actual places and people, the emotions we feel and memories we carry in our bodies. Research shows that how we feel affects what we know: the positive moods that can come with being in our bodies and alive in our senses—going for a walk or swim, enjoying nature and friends—increase our capacity to be flexible and creative in problem-solving as well as thorough in decision-making.

We believe stories are more memorable and compelling than data. A letter to yourself that includes personal narratives will re-evoke insight and understanding because you have internalised them into your own meanings, language and histories. Christine still works with plans and targets in her daily life when being a part of boards, mentoring and teaching. She keeps score so she knows who wins against the criteria that matter. Amanda rereads her letters to herself, especially before embarking on a new program or challenging opportunity. Some element—a story or suggestion to remember—is always resonant and moving. They remind us that while apprehension—even fear—is normal, good processes and people—others and yourself—should be trusted.

Acknowledgements

Our first thanks go to the thousands of women we've taught and worked with, separately and together, including on Australian New Zealand School of Government's (ANZSOG's), 'Women in Leadership: Achieving and Flourishing' program. Your experiences and openness have inspired and encouraged us to write this book about what we have learned together, in the hope it will be helpful to others—both women and men.

The book also draws on the experiences and advice of many women leaders who have joined panels and been speakers in programs, and we wish to thank them. These opportunities to hear from invited leaders are always highly rated, and they demonstrate the value of women's leadership: their willingness to share failures as well as successes, and their desire to support other women to achieve and flourish. They include but are not limited to: Helen Silver, Nicole McKechnie, Helen Szoke, Robyn Kruk, Jenny Peachey, Anne Tiernan, Bridget Hewson, Carlene York, Carmel MacGregor, Carol Schwartz, Michelle Hippolite, Naomi Ferguson, Monica Barone, Elizabeth Jack, Heather Haselgrove, Gill Callister, Jacqui Allen, the Hon. Lara Giddings, Jane Holden, Helen Gluer, Jen de Vries, Kay Rundle, Lisa Corbyn, Professor Claire Martin, Professor Sally Walker, Wendy Steendam, Tamara O'Shea, Sharon Kimberley, Sonia Cooper, Cynthia Balogh, Kerry Thompson, Sonia Cooper, Claire Austin, Jill Bond and Cathy Robinson. We've also had the benefit of hearing from and wish to thank male leaders who've articulated how and why organisations should support women in leadership, including Graeme Head, Jim Betts and John Alford.

We wish to thank friends and colleagues, including our publishers Louise Adler and Sally Heath, editor Louise Stirling and the MUP team, who encouraged us and said 'this book is going to be really helpful to many people'. Similarly, we thank the ANZSOG staff for their enthusiasm for the original idea of the Women in Leadership program, as well as for their ongoing support as the program and this book have evolved.

Thank you to our partners and families who've supported the venture of us writing this book together in big and small ways: reading drafts, being editors, sounding boards, technical advisors, unpaid finders of references and permissions, through to the most important area of cooking delicious food and putting a wineglass in our hands after a long stint at the desk. Christine would like to thank John Becquet for his love, persistence and support; her family, in particular her parents Betty and Ross Nixon, who have given her courage and resilience in spades; and her friends, who encouraged her to finish the book and contributed their wisdom. Amanda also wants to thank her partner, Warwick Pattinson, her extended family and friends, but especially Charlie, Huw, Amy and James for their love, their interest in her work (sometimes surprising but always delightful), and most importantly for regularly reminding her what matters—to go for swims and walks, to relish time with family and to be present to the richness of whatever is unfolding now. Writing this book has also prompted Amanda to reflect on and appreciate the strong women in her family, especially her mother Barbara, as they have been pioneers and encouraged her to be bold.

Notes

Introduction

1   *Lean In* is the title of Facebook CEO Sheryl Sandberg's 2013 book, which promotes her strategy for women advancing in the workplace.
2   There is a small amount of work documenting the contribution of women educational leaders; see, for example, Jill Blackmore's research, such as her 1999 book, *Troubling Women*.
3   The results of Victoria's 2016 local government elections are a case in point, with the majority of mayors in the largest regional councils now being women, see Darren Gray, 'Women in Charge in Regional Victoria', *The Age*, 18 December 2016.
4   For a review of numbers of women in parliament following the 2016 Australian election, international comparisons and the efficacy of quotas, see Sawer, 2016, 'Australia Should Look Overseas for Ideas to Increase Its Numbers of Women MPs'.
5   Angela Pippos documents this in her excellent 2017 book, *Breaking the Mould* as well as the substantial remaining hurdles for women in sport.
6   The first American woman president was Janet Rosenberg (later Jagan), who became president of Guyana in 1997. For an extensive review of women presidents and prime ministers worldwide, see Wright, 2016, 'Hillary Wouldn't Be the First Female American President'.

1 Beginnings and collaborations

1   See Amanda's articles 1997, 'The MBA Through Women's Eyes', and 2004a, 'Journey Around Leadership', for a more detailed exploration of learning from this period.
2   For example, Delahunty's exploration of those pressures on Julia Gillard in 2014, *Gravity*.
3   See Nixon's 2011, *Fair Cop*, for a detailed discussion of the speech and its impacts.
4   Nixon, 2011, p. 126.
5   Nixon, 2011, pp. 127–8.

6 Research of organisations shows that many of them have a great deal of diversity among employees but there will be little benefit in innovation or organisational culture and openness unless they recognise, support and celebrate that diversity.
7 See Hart's 2014 *Understanding Public Management*, Heifetz and Linsky's 2002 'A Survival Guide for Leaders' and Sinclair's 2007 *Leadership for the Disillusioned* on the seductiveness of the view of leadership as individual heroism.
8 Ford, 2016, *Fight Like a Girl*, p. 86.

2 Lessons from the past

1 This famed quote is from Ulrich's obscure 1976 scholarly article; it later became the title of her 2008 book.
2 See Wright, 2016, 'Hillary Wouldn't Be the First Female American President'.
3 One of the valuable outputs of this research was the online Encyclopedia of Women and Leadership, which features descriptions of the background and achievements of over 680 women in Australian public life; see www.womenaustralia.info/leaders/index.html.
4 Francis et al., 2012, *Seizing the Initiative*; Damousi et al., 2014, *Diversity in Leadership*.
5 See Bryce's 2013 Boyer Lectures for a detailed account of worldwide women's activism that resulted in a rewrite of the United Nations conventions on human rights.
6 Steinem, 2015, *My Life on the Road*.
7 Sinclair et al., 1987, *Getting the Numbers*.
8 Eisenstein, 1997, *Inside Agitators*; Burton, 1991, *The Promise and the Price*.
9 Steinem, 2015, p. 37.
10 See, for example, Huggins, 2004, 'Indigenous Women and Leadership'; Gwenda Baker, Joanne Garngulkpuy and Kathy Guthadjaka, 'Indigenous Women Leaders in Yolgnu, Australia-wide and International Contexts' in Damousi et al., 2014, pp. 39–52; Patricia Grimshaw, 'Ruby Langford Ginibi: Bundjalung historian, writer and educator' in Francis et al., 2012, pp. 315–30; Rachel Stanfield, Ray Peckham and John Nolan, 'Aunty Pearl Gibbs: Leading for Aboriginal rights' in Damousi et al., 2014, pp. 53–70.

11 See, for example, White, 2010, 'Indigenous Australian Women's Leadership'; Moreton-Robinson, 2000, *Talking Up to the White Woman*.
12 See, for example, Grimshaw's moving account of Ruby Langford Ginibi in Francis et al., 2012.
13 Baker et al., in Damousi et al., 2012.
14 Huggins, 2004.
15 See Sinclair, 'The Feminist Case for Leadership' in Damousi et al., 2014.
16 These conclusions draw on the contributions in Davis et al., 2012, *Founders, Firsts and Feminists*, and Francis et al., 2012, among other sources.
17 See Connell, 2005, *Masculinities*; Sinclair, 1998, *Doing Leadership Differently* and 2007, *Leadership for the Disillusioned* for further examples.
18 See Sinclair and Wilson, 2002, *New Faces of Leadership*.
19 The 'Destroying the Joint' movement, which mobilised online following comments made by radio presenter Alan Jones is an Australian example, see Caro, 2012. The successful online campaign for women on British banknotes in 2013 is a UK example.
20 Galbally and Bonyhady, 2016, 'Change Agents: On the Birth of the NDIS', *The Conversation*.

3 Where women are now

1 For a recent critique of the continuing preoccupation with 'fixing women', see Fox, 2017, *Stop Fixing Women*.
2 Bain/Chief Executive Women 2013, 'Creating a Positive Cycle: Critical steps to achieving gender parity in Australia'.
3 Cassells et al., 2016, 'Gender Equity Insights 2016'. The low numbers of women are particularly pronounced in corporate organisations for reasons we discuss here. There are more encouraging statistics in public sector, not-for-profit, small business and political arenas, however women are not represented in anything like the proportion they are recruited or who are successful at middle levels.
4 Metz, 2011, 'Women Leave Because of Family Responsibilities'.
5 For fascinating and rigorous analyses showing how little biology plays a role, and how much socialisation and social stereotypes

determine women and men's parenting and work opportunities, see Fine, 2011, *Delusions of Gender* and 2017b, *Testosterone Rex*.
6. Fine, 2017b.
7. Nadya Fouad, 'Leaning in, but Getting Pushed Back (and Out)', presentation to the American Psychological Association Annual Convention, Washington, DC, 7–10 August 2014.
8. Cassells et al., 2016.
9. Sandberg, 2013.
10. Crabb, 2014, *The Wife Drought*.
11. See also Fox, 2017, *Stop Fixing Women*, for further reasons to disregard these myths.
12. Crabb, 2014, p. 217.
13. Bourke, 2016, *Which Two Heads Are Better Than One?*, provides a detailed and engaging overview of this research.
14. For a clear articulation of why companies should not rely on the business case, see Fine, 2017a, 'Business as Usual?'.
15. An increasing number of large corporations have successfully gone down this path, including BHP.
16. Whelan and Wood, 2012, 'Targets and Quotas for Women in Leadership'.
17. See, for example, Sojo et al., 2016, 'Reporting Regimes, Targets and Quotas for Women in Leadership'.
18. Tyler and Fairbrother, 2013, 'Gender, Masculinity and Bushfire'.
19. See Whelan and Wood, 2012, for example.

4 Twelve lessons in leading change

1. An earlier version of these lessons written by Christine appears in Bammer, 2015, *Change!*
2. See chapter 4, 'Going Back', in Sinclair, 2017, *Leadership for the Disillusioned*.

5 Leadership in difficult times

1. Sinclair and Haines, 1993, 'Deaths in the Workplace and the Dynamics of Response'. For more on how organisational cultures can respond to difficult times more ethically, see also Sinclair, 1993, 'Approaches to Organisational Culture and Ethics'.
2. Boin et al., 2007, *The Politics of Crisis Management*, p. 140.
3. Sinclair, 2016, *Leading Mindfully*, especially chapter 9, 'Being Mindful in Crises'.

6 Influencing and enabling

1. See also Gardner, 2004, *Changing Minds*.
2. See changingminds.org/explanations/preference/social_styles.htm.
3. Cialdini, 2007, *Influence*; see also Cialdini's YouTube video 'The Science of Persuasion', which gives an account of the practical application of his principles of persuasion.
4. First published in 1532 in Italy.
5. Another body of research that influenced Amanda came from Brazilian educator Paulo Freire. In his famous 1968 book *The Pedagogy of the Oppressed*, Freire argued that education can be used to empower and liberate but that most conventional approaches to education are tools of oppression, keeping knowledge in the hands of those who've always had it.
6. It is interesting to note that these 'rules' can cause controversy, with some citing the use of them as evidence of underlying, system-overturning radicalism. For instance, Donald Trump used the fact that Hillary Clinton had drawn upon them as evidence of her unsuitability of character for the presidency.
7. Artz et al., 2016, 'Do woman ask?'
8. Freire first developed this distinction in *The Pedagogy of the Oppressed*. Amanda has also explored midwifery as a model for learning in management education and in leadership. See Sinclair, 1997, 'The MBA through Women's Eyes'; Chamberlain, et al., 2016.
9. Amanda has written extensively on the positive role bodies can play in creating presence in leadership; see, for example, Sinclair, 2005, 'Body Possibilities in Leadership', and chapter 12, 'Looking after bodies', in 2016, *Leading Mindfully*.
10. See for example, Amy Cuddy, 'Your Body Language Shapes Who You Are', Ted.com/talks/amy_cuddy_your_body_language_shapes_who_you_are.html.
11. See, for example, Bryce, 2013 Boyer Lectures; Cunliffe and Coupland, 2012.
12. In Amanda's 1998 book, *Doing Leadership Differently*, she draws on evidence showing that men's attitudes to sexism and commitment to doing something about it are more likely to be driven by direct personal interactions with and stories from female colleagues than by logic. See also Fine, 2017a, 'Business as usual.'

7 Valuing conversations

1. Adapted from Stone et al., 1999, *Difficult Conversations*; also Sinclair, 2016, *Leading Mindfully*.
2. Isaacs, 1999, *Dialogue and the Art of Thinking Together*.
3. For more on leading with less ego, see chapter 5 of Sinclair, 2016.
4. See 'Listening from Stillness' chapter in Sinclair, 2016.
5. The categories of 'politeness' and 'reflective dialogue' come from Isaacs, 1999; see also 'Dialogue for Insight' chapter in Sinclair, 2016.

8 'Hot coals' management

1. Kotter, 1990, 'What Leaders Really Do'; Kotter, 2012, *Leading Change*. For a summary of how theory has made the distinction, see Donna Ladkin, 'Leadership, Management and Headship' in Carroll et al. (eds), 2015, *Leadership*.
2. Zaleznik, 1977, 'Managers and Leaders: Are they different?'.
3. See chapter 2 in Sinclair, 2007, *Leadership for the Disillusioned*, and Sinclair, 2009, 'Seducing Leadership', for more on how management has been neglected in favour of leadership, and why.

9 Power: How to find it, use it and own it

1. See Chamberlain et al., 2016, 'Traditional Midwifery or "Wise Women" Models of Leadership'.
2. There are many eminent women philosophers, including Hannah Arendt, Iris Marion Young, Judith Butler and Luce Irigaray, who have studied power. Women are rare as theorists of leadership and power, one exception being the pioneer in organisation theory, Mary Parker Follett, whose posthumously published collection of speeches and short articles in 1942 included a chapter with the title 'Power'. See also feminists for their discussion of power, for example, Eva Cox, 1996, *Leading Women*.
3. See chapter 5, 'Working with Power' in Sinclair, 2007, *Leadership for the Disillusioned* for a fuller exploration of changing conceptions of power, also Cox, 1996, *Leading Women*.
4. Hartsock, 1983, *Money, Sex, and Power*, p. 226.
5. Kahane, 2010, *Power and Love*.
6. These questions draw on the 'Working with Power' chapter in Sinclair, 2007, and were initially developed into an exercise by our colleagues in gender and leadership work Jen de Vries and Maggie

	Leavitt. For more information see www.jendevries.com/programs/womens-leadership-development.
7	See, for example, Sakulku and Alexander, 2011, 'The Impostor Phenomenon'.
8	John Bingham, 2016, 'The Sisterhood Ceiling'.
9	In a high-profile US discrimination case, eventually won by a senior woman against her employer, it was argued that just because the woman had learned to emulate aggressive masculine models of performance to succeed, it did not mean that she was not still a victim of discrimination.
10	Fouad, 2014, 'Leaning in, But Getting Pushed Back (and Out)'.

10 Physicality: How women are seen as leaders and how they can respond

1	See Tracey Spicer, 'The Lady Stripped Bare', www.youtube.com/watch?v=PENkzh0tWJs.
2	Adewunmi, 2014, 'Male TV Presenter Wears Same Suit for a Year'.
3	Powell, 2014, 'Karl Stefanovic's Suit Experiment for Feminism Wins Plaudits'.
4	Rayner, 2010, 'The Crucifixion of Christine Nixon'.
5	For example, Summers, 2012, 'The Political Persecution of Australia's First Female Prime Minister'.
6	Gillard, 2014, *My Story*, p. 107.
7	See, for example, Sinclair, 2013, 'Can I Really Be Me?'; Summers, 2012; Delahunty, 2014, *Gravity*.
8	See Gillard, 2014; Delahunty 2014.
9	Smolovic-Jones and Jackson, 2015, 'Seeing Leadership'.
10	See, for example, Mavin et al., 2010, 'Fed up with Blair's Babes, Gordon's gals, Cameron's Cuties, Nick's Nymphets'; Mavin and Grandy, 2016, 'A Theory of Abject Appearance'.
11	Meriläinen et al., 2015, 'Headhunters and the "Ideal" Executive Body'.
12	Eagly, 2011, 'Female Leadership Advantage and Disadvantage'; Ibarra et al., 2013, 'Women Rising'.
13	Sinclair, 2011b, 'Leading with Body'.
14	For a discussion of these contemporary social media norms, see Summers, 2012; Ford, 2016, *Fight like a Girl*.
15	Hall and Donaghue, 2012, 'Nice Girls Don't Carry Knives', women also have to undertake extra 'identity work' in the transition to

leadership. See for example, Ely et al., 2011, 'Taking gender into account', Ibarra et al., 2013.
16 Sinclair, 1995, 'Sexuality in Leadership'.
17 See Nixon, 2011, *Fair Cop*, for a discussion of the speech.
18 Gillard, 2014, p. 112.
19 Bell and Sinclair, 2016, 'Bodies, Sexualities and Women Leaders in Popular Culture'.
20 Irigaray, 2002, *The Way of Love*, p. 55.
21 D'Enbeau and Buzzanell, 2013, 'Constructing a Feminist Organization's Identity in a Competitive Marketplace'; Ladkin, 2008, 'Leading Beautifully'; Ropo and Sauer, 2008, 'Dances of Leadership'.
22 Bell and Sinclair, 2014, 'Reclaiming Eroticism in the Academy'; see also chapters 12–14—'Looking after bodies', 'Tuning into the senses' and 'Finding pleasure in leadership'—in Sinclair, 2016, *Leading Mindfully*.
23 Livingston, 2016, 'Our Lady of the Pantsuit'.

11 Understanding identities, stages and transitions

1 These insights about identities are based on research that shows that all leaders, and especially perhaps women leaders, are likely to be engaged in 'identity work'—that is, in negotiating sustainable and distinctive identities given that leaders are also subject to intense pressures to conform to organisational (often masculine) norms. For more see Sinclair, 2011, 'Being Leaders'; Ely et al., 2011, 'Taking gender into account'.
2 See, for example, George, 2007, *True North*.
3 Amanda's supervisors, Alan (Foo) Davies and Graham Little at Melbourne University, in their different ways wrote and encouraged many students to see that 'leadership has a childhood', to adapt Graham's phrase.
4 For more on identities and identity work see chapter 4, 'Going back', in Sinclair, 2007, *Leadership for the Disillusioned*, and chapters 5 and 17 in Sinclair, 2016, *Leading Mindfully*.
5 For more on this and the role of emotion in insight, see Sinclair, 2016, chapter 16.
6 Women psychologists such as Jean Baker Miller and Carol Gilligan, feminist educationalists and philosophers have argued that many models of moral development have been constructed on male

	experience and privileged male values of logic and rationality over equally important values, such as care and minimising suffering.
7	For more on this, see the next chapter and Sinclair, 2016.
8	See, for example, Sheehy, 1995, *New Passages*.
9	Meister et al., 2017, 'Identities Under Scrutiny'.
10	Ibarra et al., 2013, 'Women Rising'.
11	A substantial literature explores feminism and why and how it supports some women and not others; see, for example, Greer, 1999, *The Whole Woman*. As we elaborated in chapter 10 our approach is to help women understand different experiences and to share our own, which is what seems to be most helpful for the diverse groups of women we teach.
12	A much earlier version of some of these ideas is in Sinclair, 2004a, 'Journey Around Leadership'.
13	This research was later compiled into the 1987 book *Getting the Numbers*, which Amanda co-authored with Lynne Strahan and Margaret Bowman. It was widely circulated as a kind of manual for women standing for local government, to help them know what to expect and learn strategies used successfully by other women.
14	There is extensive research evidence that successful women leaders exhibiting the same behaviours as their male counterparts are judged as equally effective but much less likeable; for example, Ibarra et al., 2013; Heilman et al., 2004, 'Penalties for Success'.
15	See Sawer, 2016, 'Australia Should Look Overseas for Ideas to Increase Its Number of Women MPs', for a review of international evidence on the success of quotas.

12 Managing and reducing risks

1	For more discussion of Heifetz and his teaching techniques, see chapter 3 in Sinclair, 2007, *Leadership for the Disillusioned*; Heifetz, 1994, *Leadership Without Easy Answers*, pp. 250–76; Parks, 2005, *Leadership Can Be Taught*.
2	Heifetz, 1994, p. 251.
3	Amanda's colleague Richard Searle has extended the metaphor to include 'the cloakroom' as a place that people retreat to when under stress or the imperative to do things differently. They may delude themselves that they are 'on the balcony' but actually they've opted out altogether.
4	See Sinclair, 2016, *Leading Mindfully*, especially chapters 5 and 17.
5	Heifetz, 1994, p. 267.

13 Resilience and renewal

1. See, for example, Gelles, 2016, 'The Hidden Price of Mindfulness Inc.'; Krupka, 2016, 'Corporate Resilience Training Works But What Are We Being Asked to Bear?'.
2. For this discussion of stress, we have drawn on several sources: Marchant, 2016, *Cure*; the work of Craig Hassed at Monash University; the work of researchers at the Centre for Compassion and Altruism Research and Education at Stanford University, including Kelly McGonigal, 2013, 'How to Make Stress Your Friend', www.ted.com/talks/kelly_mcgonigal_how_to_make_stress_your_friend; McGonigal, *The Upside of Stress*, 2015.
3. McGonigal, 2013 and 2015.
4. Sinclair, 2004b, 'Renewal'.
5. See Sinclair, 2016, *Leading Mindfully*, for summaries and references to this research.
6. Chapters in Sinclair, 2016, are devoted to each of these areas. Richard Searle, a colleague of Amanda's, has done particularly valuable work on 'Listening from Stillness' see www.searleburke.com.

14 Wise words from women

1. Delahunty, 2014, *Gravity*, p. xi.
2. Easton, 2015, 'Confidence v Being the "Ball-breaker"'.
3. See chapters on 'Feeling' in Sinclair, 2016, *Leading Mindfully*.
4. Gillard, 2014, *My Story*, p. 113.
5. ibid. p. 98.

Looking forward and sustaining

1. For more on writing, see chapter 10, 'Transforming Writing' in Sinclair, 2016, and her chapter with Donna Ladkin entitled 'Writing Through the Body'.

Bibliography

Adewunmi, Bim, 2014, 'Male TV Presenter Wears Same Suit for a Year—Does anyone notice?', *The Guardian* (Australia), 18 November, www.theguardian.com/lifeandstyle/womens-blog/2014/nov/17/male-tv-presenter-same-suit-year-female-colleagues-judged.

Albright, Madeleine, 2003, *Madam Secretary: A memoir*, Hyperion, California.

Arendt, Hannah, *On Violence*, 1970, Harvest Books, New York.

Artz, Benjamin, Amanda Goodall and Andrew Oswald, 2016, 'Do women ask?', IZA Discussion Paper, no. 10183, September.

Baird, Julia, 2004, *Media Tarts: How the Australian press frames female politicians*, Scribe Publications, Melbourne.

— 2016a, 'Power Struggle', *Harper's Bazaar*, no. 54, January/February.

— 2016b, *Victoria the Queen: An intimate biography of the woman who ruled an empire*, HarperCollins, Sydney.

Bammer, Gabriele (ed.), 2015, *Change! Combining analytic approaches with street wisdom*, Australian National University Press, Canberra.

Bell, Emma, and Amanda Sinclair, 2014, 'Reclaiming Eroticism in the Academy', *Organization*, vol. 21, no. 2, pp. 268–80.

— 2016, 'Bodies, Sexualities and Women Leaders in Popular Culture: From spectacle to metapicture', *Gender in Management: An International Journal*, vol. 31, no. 5/6.

Bingham, John, 2016, 'The Sisterhood Ceiling: How the final barrier to women reaching the top is … other women', *The Telegraph* (UK), 14 April, www.telegraph.co.uk/news/2016/04/13/the-sisterhood-ceiling-how-the-final-barrier-to-women-reaching-t/.

Blackmore, Jill, 1999, *Troubling Women: Feminism, leadership and educational change*, Open University Press, Buckingham, UK.

— 2010, 'Disrupting Notions of Leadership from Feminist Postcolonial Positions', *International Journal of Leadership in Education: Theory and practice*, vol. 13, no. 1, pp. 1–6.

— and Judyth Sachs, 2007, *Performing and Reforming Leaders: Gender, educational restructuring, and organizational change*, State University of New York Press, Albany.

Boin, Arjen, Paul 't Hart, Eric Stein and Bengt Sundelius, 2007, *The Politics of Crisis Management: Public leadership under pressure*, Blackwell Publishing, London.

Bourke, Juliet, 2016, *Which Two Heads Are Better Than One? How diverse teams create breakthrough ideas and make smarter decisions*, Australian Institute of Company Directors, Sydney.

Brooks, Rosa, 2014, 'Recline, Don't "Lean In"', *Washington Post*, 25 February, www.washingtonpost.com/blogs/she-the-people/wp/2014/02/25/recline-dont-lean-in-why-i-hate-sheryl-sandberg/.

Bryce, Quentin, 2013 Boyer Lectures: Going Back to Grassroots, ABC Radio National, www.abc.net.au/radionational/programs/boyerlectures/2013-boyer-lectures/5486344.

Burton, Clare, 1991, *The Promise and the Price: Essays on women and organisations*, Allen and Unwin, Sydney.

Buzzanell, Patrice, and Suzy D'Enbeau, 2014, 'Intimate, Ambivalent and Erotic Mentoring: Popular culture and mentor–mentee relational processes in *Mad Men*', *Human Relations*, vol. 67, no. 6, pp. 695–714.

Caro, Jane (ed.), 2012, 'Destroying the Joint: Why women have to change the world', University of Queensland Press, St Lucia.

Carroll, Brigid, Jackie Ford and Scott Taylor (eds), 2015, *Leadership: Contemporary critical perspectives*, Sage, London.

Cassells, Rebecca, Alan Duncan and Rachel Ong, 2016, 'Gender Equity Insights 2016: Inside Australia's gender pay gap', Bankwest Curtin Economics Centre and Workplace Gender Equality Agency, Gender Equity Series, no. 1, March.

Chamberlain, Catherine, Doseena Fergie, Amanda Sinclair and Christine Asmar, 2016, 'Traditional Midwifery or "Wise Women" Models of Leadership: Learning from Indigenous cultures', *Leadership*, vol. 12, no. 3, pp. 346–63.

Cialdini, Robert, 2007, *Influence: The psychology of persuasion*, Harper Business, New York.

Clinton, Hillary, 2014, *Hard Choices*, London, Simon & Schuster, New York.

Connell, Raewyn (RW), 2005, *Masculinities*, 2nd edn, University of California Press, Berkeley and Los Angeles.

Cox, Eva, 1996, *Leading Women: Tactics for making the difference*, Random House, Milsons Point.

Crabb, Annabel, 2014, *The Wife Drought*, Ebury Press, North Sydney.

Cuddy, Amy, 2015, *Presence: Bringing your boldest self to your biggest challenges*, Little Brown and Co.

— www.ted.com/talks/amy_cuddy_your_body_language_shapes_who_you_are

Cunliffe, Ann, and Christine Coupland, 2012, 'From Hero to Villain to Hero: Making experience sensible through embodied narrative sensemaking', *Human Relations*, vol. 65, no. 1, pp. 63–88.

D'Enbeau, Suzy, and Patrice Buzzanell, 2013, 'Constructing a Feminist Organization's Identity in a Competitive Marketplace: The intersection of ideology, culture, and image', *Human Relations*, vol. 66, no. 11, pp. 1447–70.

Damousi, Joy, Kim Rubenstein and Mary Tomsic (eds), 2014, *Diversity in Leadership: Australian women, past and present*, ANU Press, Canberra.

Davis, Fiona, Nell Musgrove and Judith Smart (eds), 2012, *Founders, Firsts and Feminists: Leaders in twentieth-century Australia*, Melbourne University Bookshop, print on demand.

Delahunty, Mary, 2014, *Gravity: Inside the PM's office during her last and final days*, Hardie Grant, Melbourne.

Eagly, Alice, 2011, 'Female Leadership Advantage and Disadvantage: Resolving the contradiction' in D Collinson, K Grint and B Jackson (eds), *Leadership* (vol. IV, 2005–09), Sage, London, pp. 251–72.

— and Linda Carli, 2007, 'Women and the Labyrinth of Leadership', *Harvard Business Review*, September, pp. 63–71.

Easton, Stephen, 2015, 'Confidence v Being the "Ball-breaker": Female bosses speak up', 4 November, www.themandarin.com.au/56514-women-leadership-confidence-key-even-puts-noses-joint/?pgnc=1.

Eisenstein, Hester, 1997, *Inside Agitators: Australian femocrats and the state*, Temple University Press, Philadelphia.

Ely, Robin, Herminia Ibarra and Deborah Kolb, 2011, 'Taking gender into account: Theory and design for women's leadership development program', Academy of Management Learning and Education, vol. 10, no. 3, pp. 474–93.

Evans, Michelle and Amanda Sinclair, 2016, 'Navigating the Territories of Indigenous Arts Leadership: Exploring the experiences and practices of Indigenous arts leaders', *Leadership*, vol. 12, no. 4, pp. 470–90.

Fine, Cordelia, 2011, *Delusions of Gender: How our minds and society, and neurosexism create difference*, Icon, London.

— 2017a, 'Business as Usual? The confused case for corporate gender equality', *The Monthly*, March.

— 2017b, *Testosterone Rex: Myths of sex, science, and society*, Icon, London.

Follett, Mary Parker, 1942, *Dynamic Administration: The collected papers of Mary Parker Follett*, edited by EM Fox and L Urwick, Pitman Publishing, London.

Ford, Clementine, 2016, *Fight like a Girl*, Allen & Unwin, Sydney.
Foster, Dawn, 2016, *Lean Out*, Repeater Books, UK.
Fouad, Nadya, 2014, 'Leaning in, but Getting Pushed Back (and Out)', presentation to the American Psychological Association Annual Convention, Washington, DC, 7–10 August.
Fox, Catherine, 2012, *Seven Myths about Women and Work*, New South Press, Sydney.
— 2017, *Stop Fixing Women: Why building fairer workplaces is everyone's business*, New South Press, Sydney.
Francis, Rosemary, Patricia Grimshaw and Ann Standish (eds), 2012, *Seizing the Initiative: Australian women leaders in politics, workplaces and communities*, eScholarship Research Centre, University of Melbourne.
Freire, Paulo, 1968, *Pedagogia do Oprimido*, translated in English as *The Pedagogy of the Oppressed* (1970) by Myra Bergman Rammos, Seabury Press, New York.
Galbally, Rhonda, and Bruce Bonyhady, 2016, 'On the Birth of the NDIS', *The Conversation*, podcast, 10 August, theconversation.com/change-agents-rhonda-galbally-and-bruce-bonyhady-on-the-birth-of-the-ndis-63662.
Gardner, Howard, 2004, *Changing Minds: The art and science of changing our own and other people's minds*, Harvard Business Review Press, Boston.
Gelles, David, 2016, 'The Hidden Price of Mindfulness Inc.', *New York Times*, 19 March, www.nytimes.com/2016/03/20/opinion/sunday/the-hidden-price-of-mindfulness-inc.html?smprod=nytcore-iphone&smid=nytcore-iphone-share.
George, William, 2007, *True North*, Harvard Business School Publishing, New York, 2007.
Gillard, Julia, 2016, Speech in Memory of Jo Cox, MP, London, juliagillard.com.au/articles/julia-gillard-speaks-in-memory-of-jo-cox-mp/.
— *My Story*, 2014, Knopf, Sydney.
Greer, Germaine, 1970, *The Female Eunuch*, 1st edn, MacGibbon & Kee/Paladin, London.
— 1999, *The Whole Woman*, Doubleday, London.
Hall, Lauren and Ngaire Donaghue, 2013, 'Nice girls don't carry knives: Construction of ambition in media coverage of Australia's first prime minister', *British Journal of Social Psychology*, vol. 52, no. 4, pp. 631–47.

Hart, Paul 't, 2014, *Understanding Public Management*, Palgrave Macmillan, London.
Hartsock, Nancy, 1983, *Money, Sex, and Power: Toward a feminist historical materialism*, Northeastern University Press, Boston.
— 1990, 'Foucault on Power: A theory for women?' in Linda Nicholson (ed.), *Feminism/Postmodernism*, Routledge, New York.
Hassed, Craig, 2003, *Know Thyself: The stress release programme*, Michelle Anderson Publishing, Melbourne.
— 2008, *The Essence of Health: The seven pillars of wellbeing*, Ebury Press, North Sydney.
Heifetz, Ronald, 1994, *Leadership Without Easy Answers*, Belknap Press, Boston.
—, Alexander Grashow and Marty Linsky, 2009, *The Practice of Adaptive Leadership: Tools and tactics for changing your organisation and the world*, Harvard Business School Publishing, Boston.
— and Marty Linsky, 2002, 'A Survival Guide for Leaders', *Harvard Business Review*, vol. 80, no. 6, pp. 65–74.
Heilman, Madeline, Aaron Wallen, Daniella Fuchs and Melinda Tamkins, 2004, 'Penalties for Success: Reactions to women who succeed at male gender-type tasks', *Journal of Applied Psychology*, vol. 89, no. 3, pp. 416–27.
Huggins, Jackie, 2004, 'Indigenous Women and Leadership: A personal reflection', *Indigenous Law Bulletin*, vol. 6, no. 1, pp. 5–7.
Ibarra, Herminia, Robin Ely and Deborah Kolb, 2013, 'Women Rising: The unseen barriers', *Harvard Business Review*, September.
Irigaray, Luce, 2002, *The Way of Love*, Continuum, London/New York.
Isaacs, William, 1999, *Dialogue and the Art of Thinking Together*, Random House, New York.
Kahane, Adam, 2010, *Power and Love*, Berrett-Koehler, San Francisco.
Kanter, Rosabeth Moss, 1977, *Men and Women of the Corporation*, Basic Books, New York.
Karelaia, N and L Guillén, 2014, 'Me, a Woman and a Leader: Positive social identity and identity conflict', *Organizational Behavior and Human Decision Processes*, no. 125, pp. 204–19.
Kark, Ronit, Ruth Preser and Tanya Zion-Waldoks, 2016, 'From a Politics of Dilemma to a Politics of Paradoxes: Feminism, pedagogy and women's leadership for social change', *Journal of Management Education*, DOI: 10.1177/1052562916634375.
Kegan, Robert, and Lisa Lahey, 2001, *How the Way We Talk Changes the Way We Work*, Jossey-Bass, A Wiley Company, San Francisco.

— 2009, *Immunity to Change*, Harvard Business School Press, Boston.
Kirner, Joan, and Moira Rayner, 1999, *The Women's Power Handbook: Get it, keep it, use it*, Viking, Ringwood, Victoria.
Kotter, John, 1990, 'What Leaders Really Do', *Harvard Business Review*, vol. 68, no. 3.
— 2012, *Leading Change*, Harvard Business School Press, Boston.
Krupka, Zoe, 2016, 'Corporate Resilience Training Works But What Are We Being Asked to Bear?', *The Conversation*, 22 March, http://theconversation.com/corporate-resilience-training-works-but-what-are-we-being-asked-to-bear-54827.
Ladkin, Donna, 2008, 'Leading Beautifully: How mastery, congruence and purpose create the aesthetic of embodied leadership practice', *Leadership Quarterly*, vol. 19, no. 1, pp. 31–41.
Livingston, Sonja, 2016, 'Our Lady of the Pantsuit: In praise—yes, praise!—of Hilary Clinton's style', 1 October, www.salon.com/2016/09/30/our-lady-of-the-pantsuit-in-praise-yes-praise-of-hillary-clintons-style/.
Machiavelli, Niccoló, *The Prince*, 1532.
Mackay, Hugh, *What Makes us Tick? The Ten Desires that Drive Us*, Hachette Australia, 2010.
Marchant, Jo, 2016, *Cure: A journey into the science of mind over body*, Penguin Random House, London.
Mavin, Sharon, Patricia Bryans and Rose Cunningham, 2010, 'Fed up with Blair's Babes, Gordon's Gals, Cameron's Cuties, Nick's Nymphets: Challenging gendered media representations of women political leaders', *Gender in Management: An International Journal*, vol. 25, no. 7, pp. 550–69.
—and Gina Grandy, 2016, 'A Theory of Abject Appearance: Women elite leaders' intra-gender "management" of bodies and appearance', *Human Relations*, vol. 69, no. 5.
McCann, Joy, and Janet Wilson, 2014, 'Representation of women in Australian Parliaments 2014', 9 July, www.aph.gov.au/About_Parliament/Parliamentary_Departments/Parliamentary_Library/pubs/rp/rp1415/WomanAustParl#_Toc392833823.
McGonigal, Kelly, 2013, 'How to Make Stress Your Friend', www.ted.com/talks/kelly_mcgonigal_how_to_make_stress_your_friend
— 2015, *The Upside of Stress: Why stress is good for you and how to get good at it*, Penguin Random House, New York.
McGregor, Judy, 2000, 'Stereotypes and Symbolic Annihilation: Press constructions of women at the top', *Women in Management Review*, vol. 15, nos 5/6, pp. 290–95.

Meister, Alyson, Amanda Sinclair and Karen Jehn, 2017, 'Identities Under Scrutiny: How women negotiate identity asymmetries at work', *Leadership Quarterly*, forthcoming.

Meriläinen, Susan, Janne Tienari and Anu Valtonen, 2015, 'Headhunters and the "Ideal" Executive Body', *Organization*, vol. 22, no. 1, pp. 3–22.

Metz, Isabel, 2011, 'Women Leave Because of Family Responsibilities: Fact or fiction?', *Asia Pacific Journal of Human Resources*, vol. 49, 2011, pp. 285–307.

Moreton-Robinson, Aileen, 2000, *Talking Up to the White Woman: Indigenous women and feminism*, University of Queensland Press, Brisbane.

Nixon, Christine, with Jo Chandler, 2011, *Fair Cop*, Melbourne University Publishing, Carlton, Vic.

Parks, Sharon Daloz, 2005, *Leadership Can Be Taught: A bold approach for a complex world*, Harvard Business Review Press, Boston.

Pippos, Angela, 2017, *Breaking the Mould: Taking a hammer to sexism in sport*, Affirm Press, South Melbourne.

Powell, Rose, 2014, 'Karl Stefanovic's Suit Experiment for Feminism Wins Plaudits', *Sydney Morning Herald*, 16 November, www.smh.com.au/entertainment/tv-and-radio/karl-stefanovics-suit-experiment-for-feminism-wins-plaudits-20141116-11nn4o.html.

Rayner, Moira, 2010, 'The Crucifixion of Christine Nixon', *Eureka Street*, 9 April.

— 2011, 'Gillard, Bligh and Leadership in a Crisis', *Eureka Street*, 7 January.

Ropo, Arja, and Erika Sauer, 2008, 'Dances of Leadership: Bridging theory and practice through an aesthetic approach' *Journal of Management and Organization*, vol. 14, no. 5, pp. 560–72.

Rose, Jacqueline, 2014, *Women in Dark Times*, Bloomsbury, London.

Sakulku, Jaruwan, and James Alexander, 2011, 'The Impostor Phenomenon', *International Journal of Behavioral Science*, vol. 6, no. 1, pp. 73–92.

Sandberg, Sheryl, with Nell Scovell, 2013, *Lean In: Women, work and the will to lead*, Random House/Allen Lane, New York.

Sawer, Marian, 2016 'Australia Should Look Overseas for Ideas to Increase Its Numbers of Women MPs', *The Conversation*, 25 August, theconversation.com/australia-should-look-overseas-for-ideas-to-increase-its-number-of-women-mps-63522.

Sheehy, Gail, 1995, *New Passages: Mapping your life across time*, Random House, New York.
Sinclair, Amanda, 1993, 'Approaches to Organisational Culture and Ethics', *Journal of Business Ethics*, vol. 12, no. 1, pp. 63–73.
— 1994, *Trials at the Top: Chief executives talk about men, women and the Australian executive culture*, The Australian Centre, University of Melbourne, Parkville.
— 1995, 'Sexuality in Leadership', *International Review of Women and Leadership*, vol. 1, no. 2, pp. 25–38.
— 1997, 'The MBA Through Women's Eyes', *Management Learning*, vol. 28, no. 3, pp. 313–30.
— 1998, *Doing Leadership Differently: Gender, power and sexuality in leading*, Melbourne University Press, Carlton.
— 2004a, 'Journey Around Leadership', *Discourse*, vol. 25, no. 1, pp. 7–19.
— 2004b, 'Renewal', *Mt Eliza Business Review*, vol. 7, no. 1, pp. 38–44.
— 2005, 'Body possibilities in Leadership', *Leadership*, vol. 1, no. 4, pp. 387–406.
— 2007, *Leadership for the Disillusioned*, Allen & Unwin, Crows Nest, NSW.
— 2009, 'Seducing Leadership', *Gender, Work and Organization*, vol. 16, no. 2, pp. 266–84.
— 2011a, 'Being Leaders: Identity and identity work in leadership', in A Bryman, D Collinson, K Grint, B Jackson and M Uhl-Bien (eds), *The Sage Handbook of Leadership*, Sage, London.
— 2011b, 'Leading with Body' in E Jeanes, D Knights and P Yancey Martin (eds), *Handbook of Gender, Work and Organization*, Wiley, Chichester, pp. 117–30.
— 2012, 'Not Just "Adding Women In": Women remaking leadership' in R Francis, P Grimshaw and A Standish (eds), *Seizing the Initiative: Australian women leaders in politics, workplaces and communities*, eScholarship Research Centre, University of Melbourne, pp. 15–34.
— 2013, 'Can I Really Be Me? The challenges for women leaders constructing authenticity', in D Ladkin and C Spiller (eds), *Authentic Leadership: Concepts, coalescences and clashes*, Edward Elgar, Cheltenham, pp. 239–51.
— 2014, 'On Knees, Breasts and Being Fully Human in Leadership', in D Ladkin and S Taylor (eds), *The Physicality of Leadership: Gesture, entanglement, taboo, possibilities, monographs in leadership and management*, vol. 6, Emerald, pp. 175–95.

— 2016, *Leading Mindfully: How to focus on what matters, influence for good and enjoy leadership more*, Allen & Unwin, Crows Nest.
— and Donna Larkin, 2017, 'Writing through the Body' in C Cassell, A Cunliffe and G Grady (eds), *The Sage Handbook of Qualitative Research Methods in Business and Management*, Sage.
— and Fiona Haines, 1993, 'Deaths in the Workplace and the Dynamics of Response', *Journal of Contingencies and Crisis Management*, vol. 1, no. 3, pp. 125–37.
— and Valerie Wilson, 2002, *New Faces of Leadership*, Melbourne University Publishing, Carlton, Vic.
— , Lynne Strahan and Margaret Bowman, 1987, *Getting the Numbers: Women in local government*, Hargreen Publishing in conjunction with Municipal Association of Victoria, North Melbourne.
Smolovic-Jones, Owain, and Brad Jackson, 2015, 'Seeing Leadership: Becoming sophisticated consumers of leadership' in B Carroll, J Ford and S Taylor (eds), *Leadership: Contemporary critical perspectives*, Sage, London, pp. 253–71.
Sojo, Victor, Robert Wood, Sally Wood and Melissa Wheeler, 2016, 'Reporting Regimes, Targets and Quotas for Women in Leadership', *Leadership Quarterly*, vol. 27, no. 3, pp. 519–36.
Steinem, Gloria, 2015, *My Life on the Road*, Penguin Random House, Port Melbourne, Vic.
Stone, Douglas, Bruce Patton and Sheila Heen, 1999, *Difficult Conversations: How to disucss what matters most*, Viking/Penguin, New York.
Storvik, Aagoth, and Mari Teigen, 2010, *Women on Board: The Norwegian Experience*, Friedrich Ebert Stiftung International Policy Analysis.
Summers, Anne, 1975, *Damned Whores and God's Police: The colonisation of women in Australia*, Penguin, Melbourne.
— 2012, 'The Political Persecution of Australia's First Female Prime Minister', Human Rights and Social Justice Lecture, University of Newcastle, 31 August.
Tyler, Meagan, and Peter Fairbrother, 2013, 'Gender, Masculinity and Bushfire: Australia in an international context', *Australian Journal of Emergency Management*, vol. 28, no. 2, pp. 20–25.
Tzu, Sun, *The Art of War*, 1521.
Ulrich, Laurel Thatcher, 2008, *Well-Behaved Women Seldom Make History*, Penguin Random House.

Weedon, Chris, 2002, 'Key Issues in Postcolonial Feminism: A Western perspective', *Gender Forum: An internet journal for gender studies*, no. 1, http://genderforum.org/genderealisations-issue-1-2002/.

Whelan, Jennifer, and Robert Wood, 2012, 'Targets and Quotas for Women in Leadership: A global review of policies, practices and psychological research', report of the Gender Equality Project, Centre for Ethical Leadership, Melbourne Business School.

White, Nerida, 2010, 'Indigenous Australian Women's Leadership: Stayin' strong against the postcolonial tide', *International Journal of Leadership in Education*, vol. 13, no. 1, pp. 7–25.

Wright, Clare, 2013, *The Forgotten Rebels of Eureka*, Text Publishing, Melbourne.

Wright, Robin, 2016, 'Hillary Wouldn't Be the First Female American President', *New Yorker*, 1 August.

Zaleznik, Abraham, 1977, 'Managers and Leaders: Are they different?', *Harvard Business Review*, vol. 55, pp. 67–78.

Index

Abbott, Tony, 33, 201
Aboriginal community liaison officers, 92
Abzug, Bella, 122
achievements: recording, 179, 188; taking consolation from, 188
Affirmative Action (Equal Employment for Women) Act 1986, 26
Albright, Madeleine, 161
Alinsky, Saul, 89
anti-discrimination legislation, 26
appearance: double standards, 138–9
Arendt, Hannah, 124
Australia New Zealand Policing Advisory Agency (ANZPAA), 64–5
Australian Local Government Women's Association, 26, 163
Australian and New Zealand School of Government (ANZSOG): Women in Leadership program, 4–5, 6, 192–3, 197
Avery, John, 111, 115

Baird, Julia, 141
battles: choosing, 189
Batty, Rosie, 77
Becquet, John, 7, 84
Bell, Emma, 150
Benson, Howard, 186
Bingham, John, 128
board chairs: percentage of women, 36–7

board directors: percentage of women, 36–7
Bonyhady, Bruce, 32
Borgen (Danish TV series), 150–1
borrowed protection, 94
Boston Consulting Group (BCG), 88
Bridges, William, 159
Bryce, Quentin, 22
bushfires: Black Saturday, 78–9; recovery and reconstruction, 78–85; responses of men and women to, 45, 83; Royal Commission into Black Saturday bushfires, 139–41
business case for gender diversity, 43–4, 97
Buzzanell, Patrice, 151

career planning and advancement: individual paths, 198; self-belief, 198–9
caring: for those you lead, 58–60
cartoon: sexist cartoons 142
Chandler, Jo, 4
change: distinguished from transition, 154–5
'Change Agents' (podcast), 32–3
change implementation: caring for those you lead, 58–60; fertile environment for, 60; goal-setting and accountability, 62–3; leadership capacities, development of, 65; leverage, 61–2; organisational history and, 54–6; perspective, maintaining,

65–6; reasons for change, 60–1; research, 63–5; respect for those you lead, 52–4; timing and appetites for change, 56; values, promotion of, 56–8
charismatic leadership, 30
Chattopadhyay, Kamaladevi, 25
chief executive officers (CEOs): percentage of women, 36
chief financial officers (CFOs): percentage of women, 36
chief operating officers (COOs): percentage of women, 36
Cialdini, Robert, 88
Clinton, Hillary, 22, 143, 153, 161, 221n6
Coles Variety Stores, 7, 110, 111
community activism, 33
Compstat, 63
conflict: externalising, 175–6
consensus building, 30
conversations: difficult conversations, 101–2; elements of good conversations, 104–9; emotions and, 101–2, 105–6; features of good conversation, 103–4; initiating important conversations, 101, 102–4; intent and role, 104–5; listening in, 107; reflective dialogue, 107–9; types, 100
corruption: tackling, 77–8
counterterrorism research, 64
Country Women's Association (CWA), 21–2, 163
Crabb, Annabel, 41–2, 205
crises: defining, 68–70

crisis management: crisis stages and responses, 82–3; leadership styles and, 83–5
criticism: reducing reactivity to, 176–8
Crook, Karen, 21–2
Cuddy, Amy, 96, 152
cutbacks: responding to, 71–2

Damousi, Joy, 24
D'Aprano, Zelda, 25
de Vries, Jen, 135–6, 204
death of member of organisation: responding to, 70–1
deficit model of women's leadership, 40
Delahunty, Mary, 198
D'Enbeau, Suzy, 151
'Destroying the Joint' movement, 219n19
discrimination: anti-discrimination legislation, 26; calling out, 210; 'motherhood penalty', 38–9; negotiation of pay, 39, 93–4; pay gap, 39, 167; victims of, 223n9
dishonesty: tackling, 77–8
diversity: business case for diversity 43; human capital arguments for, 44
double standards, 139
Drucker, Peter, 112

education: 'banking model' vs 'midwifery model', 95; women's levels of, 36
educational opportunities: encourage and support for, 95

ego-driven leadership, 172
Ely, Robin, 161
emergencies: defining, 68–70; responding to, 81–2
EMILY's List, 25, 163
enabling others: from women's perspective, 93–8; as leadership role, 86, 105
Encyclopedia of Women and Leadership, 218n3
energy: maintaining, 188
English suffragette movement, 24–5
equal opportunity legislation, 26
erotic leadership, 151
Eureka rebellion, 23–4
evidence-based action and programs, 94
executives: percentage of women, 35
experience: value of, 188
external stakeholders and allies, 92–3

Fair Cop, 4, 6
family: role of, 204–5
family violence: as crisis, 68; difficulty of escaping from, 180; responding to crisis of, 75–7; Victorian Royal Commission into, 18, 76, 208
fear: coping with, 179–80
feminism, 161, 162–4, 165–6, 209–10
femocrats, 26
Ferraro, Geraldine, 175, 176
financial abuse, 207–8
Follett, Mary Parker, 124

Ford, Clementine, 17
The Forgotten Rebels of Eureka (Wright), 23–4
formal authority, 124, 167
Foster, Dawn, 134
Fouad, Nadya, 38, 134
Fox, Catherine, 41
Francis, Rosemary, 24
Freire, Paulo, 221n5

Galbally, Rhonda, 32, 33, 34
Gardner, Howard, 96
Gassner, Leigh, 77
gender diversity: business case for, 43–4, 97
gender pay gap, 39, 167
gender research, 166–7
gender stereotypes: negotiation and, 93–4
gendered criticism: pre-empting, 175–6
Gibson, Jack, 171
Gillard, Julia, 33, 142, 149, 175–6, 178, 198, 200–1
Gladwell, Malcolm, 144
glass cliff, 128
goal setting: and accountability for delivery, 62–3; looking forward, 212–13
Good Shepherd Microfinance, 7, 52, 92
Grashow, Alexander, 16
Grimshaw, Patricia, 21, 24

Haines, Fiona, 70
Hartsock, Nancy, 124
heart: leading with, 199
hegemonic masculinity, 30

Heifetz, Ronald, 16, 124, 170, 171, 175, 189
heroic leadership, 16, 23, 45, 83, 166
Hite, Shere, 164
Holt, Lillian, 135
Howe, Brian, 32
Huggins, Jackie, 28–9
human capital: diversity and, 44
humour: maintaining sense of, 178, 187–8

Ibarra, Herminia, 161
identity: dynamic nature of, 155; exploring, 155–8; separating self from role, 181–2, 205; sexual identity 144, 146–8
'identity work', 224*n*1
impostor syndrome/impostorism, 126
Indian independence struggle, 25
Indigenous Australian women leaders, 27–9
indigenous women: leadership of, 27–9
influencing others: from women's perspective, 93–8; invoking authority, 88–9; leadership and, 86; personal style and, 88; political approaches, 89–93; psychological research and approaches, 87–9
institutional change *see* change implementation
intelligence: embodiment of, 213–14
international women's movements, 24–5

intimate partner relationships, 190, 204–5
intimate partner violence, 206–7
introducing yourself as a leader, 10–11
Irigaray, Luce, 151
Isaacs, William, 105

journals, 213

Kahane, Adam, 124
Kanter, Rosabeth Moss, 200
Kegan, Robert, 158–9
Kirner, Joan, 25, 122, 142
Kolb, Deborah, 161
Kotter, John, 112

Lahey, Lisa, 158–9
leadership: changing assumptions about, 167; flourishing in, 119–20; formal authority and, 124; improving opportunities for women, 46–8; management and, 112; myths about, 170–1; reasons for increasing women's representation, 44–6; why and how bodies matter in, 143–5; women-centred understandings, 171
leadership capacities: developing, 65, 95
Leadership and Change MBA: class format, 15–16
leadership culture: assumptions, 41–3
leaning in, 36, 132–4, 136, 161; but getting pushed out, 38, 134

leaning out, 134, 136
'less ego' leadership; 167
Linsky, Marty, 16
listening, 107, 174–5
local government: women in, 25–6, 163–4, 217*n*3, 225*n*13
lone warrior myth, 170–1

McGonigal, Kelly, 185
Machiavelli, Niccoló, 89
Mackay, Hugh, 87, 157
Macklin, Jenny, 33
management: importance of good managers, 117–18; leadership and, 112; qualities of good managers, 113–17
management skills: improving, 65
meaning systems, 158–9
meditation, 182, 194
Meister, Alyson, 160
Melbourne Business School: barriers to women completing MBA programs, 165
men: attitudes to sexism, 221*n*12; improving opportunities for women, 46–7
mentors, 204
Merrill, David, 88
middle managers: percentage of women, 36
midwifery, 221*n*8
mindfulness, 194–6
Monash University: counterterrorism unit, 64
Moore, Mark, 55
moral development models 224–5*n*6
motherhood penalty, 38

moving on, 180–1
Muirhead, Tim, 136

National Council of Women (NCW), 24, 30
National Disability Insurance Scheme (NDIS), 31, 32–4
negotiation: gender stereotypes and, 93–4
networks: drawing on, 94
Nixon, Christine: as Assistant Commissioner in NSW Police, 92; background and career, 6–7, 51–2, 110; as Chair of Bushfire Reconstruction and Recovery Authority, 7, 51, 79, 84–5, 181; as Chair of Good Shepherd Microfinance, 7, 52, 92, 187; as Chair of Monash College, 7, 52; on change implementation, 52–66; as Chief Commissioner of Victoria Police, 11, 14–15, 51, 53–4, 56–8, 116, 180–1; commitment to women's equality and advancement, 7–8; as Deputy Chancellor of Monash University, 7, 52; leadership roles, 3, 5, 7; on management, 111–12, 113; media portrayals of, 139–41, 142–3; on partnerships, 173–4; as Police Region Commander, south coast of NSW, 3, 14; Pride March participation, 58–9; swearing-in as Police Commissioner, 11, 56–8, 149; on violence against women, 206–9; work with Amanda Sinclair, 4, 17, 174–5

norms: shaping, 12–16
NSW Police Association: Women's Branch, 91, 189–90

Obama, Michelle, 210
O'Donoghue, Lowitja, 28
organisational failures: responding to, 73–5
organisational history: understanding, 54–6
organised crime, 88
outside interests, 182
Overland, Simon, 173

partnerships: between women, 17–18; finding and working with, 173–5; identifying partners, 18; importance for leaders, 16–18, 203–4; institutional structures and, 18
pay gap, 39, 167
pay rates: negotiation of, 39, 93–4
personal barriers, 201–2
personal risks, 170
personal style, 88
perspective: gaining, 171–2; maintaining, 65–6
physical presence, 96
Pilkington, Doris, 28
Plan International, 209
police corruption, 69, 77, 93
police violence, 77–8
policing: women's organisations influence on, 24
political leaders: women's contributions as, 22
political smarts: developing, 92

power: definition in masculine terms, 122; exercising and owning, 134–7; informal sources, 121; new conceptions of, 123–5; 'power-over' vs 'power-with', 124; sources, 121–2, 130–4; women's ambivalence towards, 121
powerlessness: experiencing and overcoming, 125–30
problem-solving, 102, 171
professional risks, 169
public value: creating, 55
purpose: clarity about, 190–1; staying connected to, 178–9
Putin, Vladimir, 144

Queen Bee syndrome, 128
quotas, 44, 167

radical feminism, 164
Rayner, Moira, 122, 139, 142
redundancies: responding to, 71–2
reflective dialogue, 107–9
relaxation response, 186
renewal: need for, 191–4
research: importance in change implementation, 63–5; use of, 94
resilience, 187–91, 201–2
resistance: responding to, 176–8
respect: self-respect, 191; for those you lead, 52–4
restructuring: responding to, 71–2
ridicule: responding to, 91
risk-taking, 202
risks: key sources, 170–1
Roosevelt, Franklin D, 144

Rosenberg, Janet, 22
rules and procedures:
    understanding, 189–90
'Rules for Radicals', 89

Sandberg, Sheryl, 132–3, 161, 204
Scott, Evelyn, 28
second adulthood, 160
second-wave feminism, 164
self-authorisation, 90
self-authorising mind stage, 159
self-belief, 198–9
self-care, 184
self-compassion and forgiveness, 202
self-reflection, 201–2
self-respect, 191, 203
self-transforming mind stage, 159
senior management roles: absence/exclusion of women, 37–40, 165; proportion of women in, 26–7
sexism, 149, 152, 221n12
sexist cartoons, 142
sexist double standards, 139
sexual identity: sexualities in leadership 144, 146–8
sex-segregated work environments, 165
shared leadership, 30
Sheehy, Gail, 159, 160
Shorten, Bill, 32
Sinclair, Amanda: background and career, 3–4, 8–9, 110, 162–6; commitment to supporting women's leadership, 8, 166–7; feminism, 162–6; gender research, 166; as lecturer at Melbourne Business School, 165, 166; teaching, 15; research, 43, 135, 137, 144, 146 155–6, 163, 166; as social planner, 164–5; transitions 162–7; work with Christine Nixon, 4, 17, 174–5; on writing 212, 213–14; yoga teaching, 155, 174, 182, 191, 212
socialised mind stage, 158
Sonnenfeld, Jeffery, 180
Spicer, Tracey, 138, 146
sponsors, 204
spousal abuse, 190, 206
Stefanovic, Karl, 139
Steinem, Gloria, 25, 27
stolen motor vehicles, 73–4
Stone, Douglas, 101
storytelling, 96, 214
stress: causes and responses to, 185–7
stress management, 183, 202
suffragette tactics, 25
Summers, Anne, 142
Sun Tzu, 89

't Hart, Paul, 16, 82
talking circles, 27
Tannen, Deborah, 140
'targets with teeth', 44
Tolhurst, Kevin, 79
transitions: distinguished from change, 154–5; enabling, 158–61
Trump, Donald, 221n6
Tyler, Meagan, 45

values: discussing and establishing, 12–16; promotion of, 56–8; reiterating, 178–9
Victoria Police: accountability, 62–3; alcohol policy, 176–7; Armed Offenders Squad, 77–8, 106, 177; Crime Department reform, 173; crime rates, reducing, 61–2, 73–5; cultural change, approach to, 61–2; drug squad corruption, 69; external pressures for change, harnessing, 56, 93; governance, 15; legitimacy and capability, 56; managers, development of, 65; organisational history, 54–6; reform process, engaging members in, 14–15, 53–4; research commissioned, 64–5; station-building program, 59
Victorian Bushfire Appeal Fund, 79
Victorian Bushfire Reconstruction and Recovery Authority (VBRRA), 79–80
violence against women, 206–9

Warren Harding Effect, 144
Watson, Emma, 209–10
Whelan, Jennifer, 44
Wilkinson, Lisa, 139
women: changes in self-perception, 161; changes in treatment over lifetime, 160–1; lack of support from other women, 128–30; pretending to be men, 189
women leaders: multiple pressures on, 145; personal risks, 170; professional risks, 169; responding to visibility and bodily stereotypes, 145–53; supporting other women, 161–8, 206–9; understanding challenges of, 200–1; visibility and scrutiny of, 139–43
women leaders in history: features of women's leadership, 29–31; lack of acknowledgment of, 22–3; learning from, 23–5
Women in Leadership program, 4–5, 6, 10, 192–3, 197
Women's Co-ordination Unit (NSW), 26
Women's Electoral Lobby (WEL), 25, 26, 163
women's leadership: features of, 29–31, 46; judged on basis of appearance, 139–43; telling stories of, 31–4
Wood, Robert, 44
workplaces, sex-segregated environments, 165
workplace participation: women, 36, 37
Wright, Clare, 23–4
writing: value of, 212, 213–14

yoga, 155, 174, 182, 183, 186, 191, 212